English Romantic Poets

Selections from the Poems of

WILLIAM WORDSWORTH

Selections from the Poems of WILLIAM WORDSWORTH

Edited by A. Hamilton Thompson, M.A., F.S.A.

CAMBRIDGE
AT THE UNIVERSITY PRESS
1959

CAMBRIDGE
UNIVERSITY PRESS

University Printing House, Cambridge CB2 8BS, United Kingdom

Cambridge University Press is part of the University of Cambridge.

It furthers the University's mission by disseminating knowledge in the pursuit of education, learning and research at the highest international levels of excellence.

www.cambridge.org
Information on this title: www.cambridge.org/9781107544659

First edition 1917
Reprinted 1921, 1924, 1926, 1959
First paperback edition 2015

A catalogue record for this publication is available from the British Library

ISBN 978-1-107-54465-9 Paperback

PREFACE

AS in the previous volumes of this series, the poems have been arranged in their approximately chronological order. The selections from *The Prelude* and *The Excursion*, however, the composition of which extended over a considerable number of years, have been placed at the end of the book. These two poems are the completed portions of a work to which Wordsworth intended his miscellaneous verse to be subsidiary, and it is hoped that the passages which it has been found possible to include will serve to illustrate his design and to manifest the unity of their contents with those of the pieces which precede them. The aim which has guided the editor in the work of selection has been to shew as clearly as possible the spirit which animates Wordsworth's poetry, his perception of an inward presence in all Nature, communicating itself to man's apprehension and acting as a fortifying and restraining influence, at once a source of content and an impulse to right action. A few of the more famous lyrics, e.g. the *Elegiac Stanzas* on Sir

George Beaumont's picture of Peele Castle, and *The Happy Warrior*, which are to be found in almost every anthology, have been omitted to make room for pieces less familiar, but not less striking. The various sources which have been consulted for the purpose of this volume will be found mentioned in the notes: for the chronological sequence of the poems the editor has depended largely upon the one volume editions by Lord Morley of Blackburn and Mr Thomas Hutchinson. As in other volumes of selections, he has been aided greatly by the advice of his wife, who has read and given help with the notes.

A. H. T.

Gretton,
Northants.
May 1917

CONTENTS

PRINCIPAL DATES IN THE LIFE OF WORDSWORTH

1770, 7 April.	Born at Cockermouth, Cumberland.
1771, 25 Dec.	Birth of Dorothy Wordsworth.
1778.	Enters Hawkshead grammar school, Westmorland.
1783.	Death of his father, John Wordsworth.
1785.	Composition of his earliest poem now known to exist, *Lines written as a school exercise at Hawkshead* on the second centenary of the foundation of the school.
1787.	Goes into residence at St. John's college, Cambridge.
1790, summer.	Visits France with Robert Jones, walking through France and Switzerland to the lake of Como.
1791, Jan.	Takes his B.A. degree and leaves Cambridge.
1791, Nov.-1792.	Residence in France: visits Paris and stays at Orléans and Blois.
1792, Oct.	Returns to England, and leads a restless and unsettled life, without a permanent home till 1795.
1793.	Publication of *An Evening Walk. An Epistle; in Verse* (written 1787-9), followed by *Descriptive Sketches,* a memorial of the tour of 1790, written in France, 1791-2.
1795.	Receives a legacy of £900 from Raisley Calvert.
1795, Oct.	Settles at Racedown, Dorset, with Dorothy Wordsworth. First meeting with Coleridge at Bristol about this time.
1797, June.	Coleridge visits Racedown.

1797, July.	The Wordsworths visit Coleridge at Nether Stowey, Somerset, and remove from Racedown to Alfoxden, near Stowey.
1798, Sept.	Publication of *Lyrical Ballads*, the result of collaboration with Coleridge. The Wordsworths leave Alfoxden and go to Germany with Coleridge and John Chester on 14 Sept. From 6 Oct. they make their head-quarters at Goslar in Hanover.
1799, April.	Return to England, after a short visit to Coleridge at Göttingen.
1799, May-Oct.	Residence at Sockburn, co. Durham, with his cousins, the Hutchinsons.
1799, Oct., Nov.	Tour in the Lake country with John Wordsworth, Coleridge and Joseph Cottle.
1799, Dec.	Settles, with Dorothy Wordsworth, at Dove cottage, Grasmere.
1801, Jan.	Publication of *Lyrical Ballads*, 2d ed., in two vols. (dated 1800) with preface explaining Wordsworth's theory of poetry. 3d ed., 1802; 4th ed., 1805.
1802, 21 May.	First sonnets written.
1802. 9 July.	Leaves Grasmere with Dorothy for Yorkshire. They go from Yorkshire to London, spend Aug. at Calais, and are in London again, 30 Aug.-22 Sept.
1802, 4 Oct.	Marries Mary Hutchinson (born 16 Aug., 1770) at Brompton-in-Pickering-lythe, Yorks. They return to Grasmere, 6 Oct.
1803, 18 June.	Birth of Wordsworth's eldest son, John.
1803, 14 Aug.-25 Sept.	Tour in Scotland with Dorothy and Coleridge, with Dorothy alone after 29 Aug. First visit to Scott, 17 Sept.
1804, 16 Aug.	Birth of Dora Wordsworth.
1805.	Completes *The Prelude*, begun 1799-1800, continued 1804-5, published 1850.

1806, Oct.	Removes temporarily from Grasmere to Coleorton, Leices.
1806, Dec.-1807, Feb.	Coleridge visits Coleorton.
1807.	Publication of *Poems in Two Volumes*.
1807, Aug.	Wordsworth returns to Grasmere.
1808, June.	Removes from Dove cottage to Allan Bank, Grasmere.
1809, May.	Publication of pamphlet *Concerning the Relations of Great Britain, Spain, and Portugal, to each other, and to the common enemy, at this Crisis,* upon the convention of Cintra.
1810, April.	Publication of *Description of the Scenery of the English Lakes* (introduction to Thomas Wilkinson's *Select Views in Cumberland,* etc.: published separately 1822).
1810, Oct.	Beginning of estrangement from Coleridge, due to the tactlessness of Basil Montagu, and lasting till May, 1812.
1811.	Removes from Allan Bank to the Rectory, Grasmere.
1812, 4 June.	Death of Catherine Wordsworth, second daughter (born 6 Sept. 1808); followed, 1 Dec., by death of Thomas, second son (born 16 June, 1806).
1813, March.	Appointed stamp-distributor for Westmorland. Removes from Grasmere rectory to Rydal Mount, his home for the rest of his life.
1814, July.	Second tour in Scotland, with his wife and Sara Hutchinson.
1814, Aug.	Publication of *The Excursion*, begun 1802, written chiefly 1809-13.
1815, March.	Publication of *Poems by William Wordsworth,* 2 vols., a collected edition of all his published poems except *The Excursion,* classified under specific headings.

1815, May.	Publication of *The White Doe of Rylstone*, begun on a visit to Stockton-on-Tees in Dec., 1807.
1816.	Publication of *Thanksgiving Ode, Jan.* 18, 1816, *with other short pieces.*
1819, Apr., May.	Publication of *Peter Bell, a tale in verse*, and *The Waggoner, a Poem.*
1820, May.	Publication of *The River Duddon, a series of sonnets.* Leaves Rydal Mount with his wife and sister for visit to London and continental tour.
1820, July.	Publication of *Miscellaneous Poems*, 4 vols., a collected edition, excluding *The Excursion*, of which a 2nd ed. appears this year.
1820, 11 July-Nov.	Tour to Switzerland and the Italian Lakes. Returns to Rydal Mount, 24 Dec.
1822.	Publication of *Memorials of a Tour on the Continent*, 1820, and *Ecclesiastical Sketches*, afterwards called *Ecclesiastical Sonnets.*
1823, May, June.	Tour in the Netherlands.
1824, Aug.-Oct.	Tour in Wales.
1827.	Publication of *Poetical Works*, 5 vols., including *The Excursion*, with dedication to Sir George Beaumont of Coleorton (d. Feb. of this year).
1828, June.	Tour on the Rhine with Dora Wordsworth and Coleridge.
1829, Aug., Sept.	Tour in Ireland.
1831, Sept., Oct.	Tour in Scotland with Dora and his nephew Charles, visiting Scott at Abbotsford on the way.
1832.	Publication of *Poetical Works*, 4 vols.
1833, Sept., Oct.	Tour in Isle of Man and Scotland with his eldest son (rector of Moresby, Cumberland) and Crabb Robinson.
1834, 25 July.	Death of Coleridge.
1835.	Publication of *Yarrow Revisited and other poems.*

1835, Aug.-Nov.	Stays with Thomas Hutchinson at Brinsop court, near Hereford.
1836-7.	Publication of *Poetical Works*, 6 vols.
1837, March-Aug.	Tour in France and Italy with Crabb Robinson.
1838, June.	Publication of *Sonnets* in collected edition.
1838.	Receives D.C.L. degree at Durham.
1839, July.	Receives D.C.L. degree at Oxford.
1841, Apr.-Aug.	Visits West of England and places associated with his early poems. Marriage of Dora Wordsworth and Edward Quillinan at Bath, 11 May (Dora died 9 July, 1847).
1842, April.	Publication of *Poems, chiefly of early and late years*, including *The Borderers* and other unpublished pieces (added as vol. 7 to *Poetical Works*). Resigns his stamp-distributorship in July, and receives an annual pension of £300 from the civil list in Oct.
1843, 21 March.	Death of Southey.
1843, April.	Appointed Poet laureate.
1845.	Publication of collected *Poems*, 1 vol.
1847, 6 July.	Ode celebrating the installation of Prince Albert as chancellor of the University performed in the Senate house, Cambridge.
1849-50.	Publication of *Poetical Works*, 6 vols., with revised text.
1850, 23 April.	Death of Wordsworth. Buried at Grasmere, 27 April.
1850.	Publication of *The Prelude* (vol. 8 of *Poetical Works*: for vol. 7 see 1842).

INTRODUCTION

LIKE Milton, to whose influence he owed much that was best in his work, Wordsworth belongs to that chosen band of poets to whom poetry is a priesthood, demanding a special consecration and undisturbed devotion. His life was spent in the exercise of his natural gift, in daily intimacy with its inspirer, Nature. Although, at a critical period, he was tempted to follow Milton's example and take an active part in the strife for political liberty, his destiny ruled otherwise. His part in the movements of his age was the liberation of poetry from convention. In this he did not stand alone. Other poets brought a diversity of gifts to the same task. But Wordsworth's interpretation of the inner meaning of Nature, which became his life's mission, was a thing by itself. It was his peculiar achievement to reveal the invisible impulses at work behind the outward beauty of Nature, and to manifest her sustaining influence upon the spirit of man.

The association of human emotion with natural objects was brought home to him early in life. The music of his native river, the Derwent, gave him

> A foretaste, a dim earnest, of the calm
> That Nature breathes among the hills and groves.

In his schooldays at Hawkshead, the mountains lay round him 'like giants at a hunting,' their stillness broken by whisperings of other and mightier presences, on which, in his moonlit wanderings, he trembled to intrude. He learned instinctively that fear which is inseparable from the love of Nature: his passion for her external charm was checked and disturbed by momentary revelations of her hidden power, 'gleams like the flashings of a shield,' which transfigured sensible objects and awakened doubts as to their reality. When, in later years, he was able to understand these visitations, he was disposed to regard the state in which they were still obscure as one of blind devotion to the concrete allurements of sight and sound. But there was no time at which those

> notes that are
> The ghostly language of the ancient earth,
> Or make their dim abode in distant winds

ceased to stir him with their mystery. His point of view underwent no sudden revolution. Confident calm in process of time took the place of vague terrors: the hauntings of invisible forces still thrilled him with reverence, but he regarded them with perfect trust and understanding.

Communion with Nature, however, pursued as a solitary enjoyment, could not by itself awaken his poetic genius. During his residence at Cambridge, where he associated freely with his contemporaries, indulging in what he severely described as a 'heartless chase of trivial pleasures' and shewing no signs of exclusive dedication to the service of poetry, he was attracted by new and wider interests. Human society exercised its definite claims upon him. The outbreak of the French revolution moved him with enthusiasm for the prospect of human liberty. In the long vacation of 1790, he landed at Calais on the eve of the anniversary of the fall of the Bastille. Everywhere joy was manifest,

> France standing on the top of golden hours,
> And human nature seeming born again.

Wordsworth was in complete sympathy with the ambitions of the new era. Returning to France in November, 1791, he identified himself with the liberal patriots whose aim was the overthrow of tyranny and the reign of reason and nature, and he even contemplated taking an active part in the councils of the Girondins. Fortunately for poetry, he abandoned a scheme which in all probability would have been fatal to him. When he came back to England in October 1792, it was still with unabated confidence in revolutionary principles, but with apprehensions raised by a visit to Paris while the memory of the September massacres was fresh. The successive acts of the drama which rapidly unfolded itself perplexed and depressed him. He felt shame for his country, the fatherland of Milton and the home of liberty, when she joined the war against the nascent French republic. France, goaded into madness by the coalition of the European powers, became the scene of 'domestic carnage.' With the fall of Robespierre,

Wordsworth's hopes revived. The news reached him one summer evening on the sands of Morecambe bay, and he then and there hailed the end of the Terror and the new reign of righteousness and peace with 'a hymn of triumph.' Once more, however, England disappointed him: her anti-revolutionary panic seemed to him a menace to justice and liberty, of which France, though stained with the blood of her own children, was still the champion. But, if he had lost faith in his own country, the course of affairs in France was to disillusion him still more. Her war of self-defence expanded into a war of conquest: she lost sight of her ideal and began to threaten the independence of her smaller neighbours. The swift transformation of the republic into a conquering empire was to Wordsworth a catastrophe less bearable than the excesses of the revolution. He was left to console himself with the mere idea of liberty, to be evoked from the study of the law of nations and the framework of society. This barren comfort drove him to confess moral problems insoluble and to take refuge in the conviction that man is governed by necessity. His reliance upon reason was shaken, and for a time he sought to restore it by leaving questions of space and time and turning to abstract science. Gradually he recognised that his heart

> had been turned aside
> From Nature's way by outward accidents

and that he was steadily losing his way as he entangled

himself in fruitless speculations alien to Nature's intentions. It was at this point that Nature again began to exercise her undivided mastery over him and to lead him to 'genuine knowledge, fraught with peace.'

He ascribed this return to confidence largely to the influence of his sister Dorothy, his constant companion from 1795, who, unsaddened by disillusion, retained the enthusiasm for natural beauty which had filled his own mind in early youth. In her he had always before him the spectacle of a mind dedicated to the service of Nature without distraction, and from her he learned the value of the inward freedom of the soul, the guarantee of genuine liberty. He spoke without reserve of his debt to her:

> She gave me eyes, she gave me ears;
> And humble cares, and delicate fears;
> A heart, the fountain of sweet fears;
>   And love, and thought, and joy.

In his quiet life with her at Racedown he found his incentive to that poetic activity which woke into vigorous life during the epoch of his association with Coleridge. At Alfoxden and Grasmere, and in the wanderings of which her *Journals* preserve a minute and accurate record, her devoted companionship was his constant support and inspiration.

His friendship with Coleridge was no less fruitful. The characters of the two poets were entirely different. There could be no greater contrast than that which existed between Wordsworth's single-minded devotion to his poetic mission and the restlessness of intellect and infirmity of will which hindered Coleridge from achieving the full promise of his early hopes. But Wordsworth and Coleridge were closely akin in sympathy. They shared the passion for liberty, they had felt the influence of the political movements of their day with equal aspirations, and they were at one in their recognition of the power of Nature. During their year of intimate communion among the Quantocks, Wordsworth and his sister gave Coleridge that sympathy and perfect understanding which he needed for the development of his poetic faculty; while Coleridge, with his store of knowledge and range of interests extended the scope of Wordsworth's imagination. *Lyrical Ballads*, the fruit of their complete intellectual union, marked a revolution in English poetry. The revolution, it is true, was not sudden. The way had been prepared for it by poets who, in an era of artificial and conventional forms, had found guidance in Nature. Wordsworth and Coleridge, however, were the first to formulate definite poetic theories in contrast to the prevailing tenets of the age, and to illustrate them in practice. Their work marked the conscious attainment of the aim towards which their predecessors, expressing personal tastes and inclinations, had been moving less consciously; and with *Lyrical Ballads* the Romantic movement in poetry came into full existence.

Of Coleridge's part in *Lyrical Ballads* something has been said in another volume of the series. Wordsworth's contributions included nothing so obviously striking as *The Ancient Mariner*, with its application of human interest to a fantastic and supernatural subject. His object, as Coleridge says, was 'to give the charm of novelty to things of every day, and to excite a feeling analogous to the supernatural, by awakening the mind's attention from the lethargy of custom, and directing it to the loveliness and wonders of the world before us.' His method of handling these every-day subjects was a direct challenge to traditional usage. The poets of the eighteenth century had fallen into habits of style which, employed to excess, had become monotonous. An elevated type of language, for which the great example of Milton was in some degree responsible, was used indiscriminately by all writers of verse. Personifications of abstract qualities, the general formulas which took the place of the description of Nature in detail, became the stock-in-trade of every pretender to poetry. A formal diction which, used to clothe real genius, was imposing and august, and, applied to witty and satiric verse, had a dazzling effect, suffered from obvious limitations. In the hands of innumerable imitators, it became pompous and ridiculous: its conventional phrases, repeated again and again, were soon trite and meaningless. Pope had advised mankind as a whole to follow Nature; but Nature in his vocabulary meant taste and correctness, the avoidance of extravagance and bathos. His followers soon shewed that, in poetry at any rate, it was difficult to avoid extremes. The path of correctness was too narrow: it prescribed the use of certain forms of which the excess was turgidness, the defect meanness. Against this limited theory of poetic style Wordsworth raised his protest and urged the following of Nature in a wider and truer sense. Nature was to be found, not in abstract definitions of the sublime and beautiful, but in ordinary life and in man's natural surroundings. In *Lyrical Ballads* his object was 'to keep the Reader in the company of flesh and blood,' and, in so doing, his 'purpose was to imitate, and, as far as possible, to adopt the very language of men.' He deprecated the use of a special poetic diction, 'vague, glossy, and unfeeling,' remote from daily language. His choice of subject was as simple as possible. The objects which environed his retired and frugal life were sufficient for him. To keep his eye steadily fixed upon his subject and to describe it plainly and without falsehood were the aims which he set before himself.

Lyrical Ballads was thus an experiment founded upon a clearly defined theory. Wordsworth confessed that he avoided 'what is usually called poetic diction' as carefully as others took pains to produce it; and, in bringing his 'language near to the language of men,' his simplicity ran the risk of becoming excessive. Those who know best the value of his poetry will not deny that his style has frequent moments in which it is of an almost infantile baldness, a fault which was readily fastened upon by contemporary critics and parodists. The ridicule which assailed the long deferred *Peter Bell*, his most self-conscious effort in every-day realism, while it overlooked the true merits of the poem, was justified to some extent by Wordsworth's insistence upon trivial details in terms which are themselves trivial and ungraceful. Humour, with the sense of proportion which it implies, is necessary to the minute description of common things; and Wordsworth lacked humour altogether. For this reason, his endeavour to prove that the language of simple prose could be used effectively for poetic purposes was partially unsuccessful. He was without the touchstone which would have enabled him to distinguish between what is merely prose and prose heightened into poetry; and throughout his life the poetic charm with which he freely invested the commonest things was constantly broken by passages in which his verse unconsciously sank to the most prosaic level.

To allow this fact, which would be enough to ruin the reputation of a lesser poet, is only to recognise more fully the greatness of Wordsworth's poetic achievement Coleridge saw clearly the fallacy which underlay Wordsworth's disclaimer of a special diction for poetry. The heightened emotion which distinguishes poetry from prose, the rhythmical arrangement of words which it naturally produces, the metrical forms which are accidents of poetry and its rhythm, necessarily mould the language of poetry into a shape essentially different from that of the language of ordinary speech. Wordsworth's poetry was the confutation of his own theory.

Where it sinks into prose, the difference is at once apparent. Where it is on its true level, the peculiar style of the individual poet is unmistakable. Simplicity of subject, truth of description, are not in themselves prosaic. In his choice and development of subject the poet is guided by his personal emotion. He feels more than he sees: his imagination is brought to bear upon his subject, and the very fact of imagination works a subtle change in the simplest style. Imagination often clothes prose with poetic beauty, but it unfailingly saves poetry from depression into prose. No one was more conscious than Wordsworth of the virtue of imagination: no poet has given more striking proof of his possession of the quality. *Peter Bell*, where his imagination was unequal, contains a classical definition of the attitude of the unimaginative man to the common beauties of Nature:

> A primrose by the river's brim
> A yellow primrose was to him
> And it was nothing more.

But to Wordsworth

> The meanest flower that blows can give
> Thoughts that do often lie too deep for tears.

Here lies the difference between the prosaic and poetic attitude to life and Nature, the difference whose outward and visible signs it was impossible to remove by any theory of the identity of the language of every-day life with that of poetry. Wordsworth, walking on the bank of Ullswater, sees a host of daffodils waving in the breeze beside the rippling waters of the lake. He recalls them in memory as

> They flash upon that inward eye
> Which is the bliss of solitude.

The language of his stanzas is simplicity itself, but it is simplicity to which emotion and imagination have given a special cast and distinction of their own. Even if we discount the metre and rhyme into which this language falls so easily and naturally, it is language of an entirely individual stamp, remote from the prose of common life.

Lines composed a few miles above Tintern Abbey, published as part of *Lyrical Ballads* in 1798, is the epitome of the lessons which Wordsworth's early experience had taught him and of the spiritual progress afterwards described at full length in *The Prelude*. If he took pains to avoid a stereotyped poetic diction and clothe his most intimate thoughts in simple language, his simplicity had at any rate a dignity and elevation which prove that the poet cannot divest himself of his singing-robes. *Tintern Abbey*, indeed, links itself in more than one respect to the verse of the generation which was passing. Its blank verse is the poetic medium inherited from Milton, the medium employed by Thomson in *The Seasons*, the most famous nature-poem of the eighteenth century, and more recently by Cowper, who among Wordsworth's fore-runners had the temperament most nearly akin to his own. Its descriptive phraseology is as conventional as that of any eighteenth-century poet: the scene of rock, wood and river was without those special qualities which called forth Wordsworth's peculiar powers of description, and there is nothing but the title of the poem to guide us to the place which inspired its composition. But, if its setting has these traditional features, its substance is entirely novel. Earlier poets may have felt these things: Gray, for example, in his tours among scenery which in his day was highly unfashionable, saw much that lay beneath the externals of Nature; but none had expressed them clearly. *Tintern Abbey* formulates the doctrine of a new age. Nature is no longer an attractive arrangement of form and colour and sound, alluring the senses. Her beauty is merely the visible symbol of a divine and all-pervading personality, living and watchful, harmonising the manifold discord of the elements that compose the forms in which it makes its home, communicating its presence at every point to those who are ready and willing to see and learn, ministering help and encouragement, and supplying a perpetual fund of strength to spirits perplexed by earthly cares.

It is this in-dwelling of Nature within the heart of man which is the cardinal principle of Wordsworth's natural religion. The Nature which he had at once feared and loved in his boyhood was a mysterious personality with which his intercourse was fitful and imperfect, a teacher half-understood, apart from himself. In his early manhood, distracted by other influences, he had lost sight of her. Man and his urgent needs had occupied the first place in his mind. But when, oppressed by the contradictions which had disappointed his hopes, he returned to his former sources of interest, he found Nature waiting for him with a new meaning. His apparent alienation from her had been merely a means to draw him to her more closely. In the interval he had cultivated that sympathy with mankind which, in his boyish pursuit of her, he had neglected. The din of the world now resolved itself into ' the still sad music of humanity,' harmonised by the eternal presence of Nature as the comforter and consoler. The passion and rapture of inexperience were gone: the melancholy of life had dimmed ' the glory and the gleam ' of early impressions; but, in the place of thoughtless joys and visionary ambitions, there had come a calm intelligence and clear-sightedness in which the past was understood and the future awaited with confidence. The state of mind in which Wordsworth's mature poetry was written is defined with his highest imaginative power in the most beautiful lines of *Intimations of Immortality:*

> Hence in a season of calm weather
> Though inland far we be,
> Our Souls have sight of that immortal sea
> Which brought us hither,
> Can in a moment travel thither,
> And see the Children sport upon the shore,
> And hear the mighty waters rolling evermore.

Poetry written in this spirit of calm, poetry which is

'the harvest of a quiet eye,' cannot but have its superficially monotonous and unattractive intervals. The vision of the 'immortal sea' is not always present: duty and the common things of life have claims which are too insistent for a sustained magnificence of style. Wordsworth, it is true, made deliberate choice of a retired life in circumstances which were highly favourable to the undisturbed cultivation of verse. But the subjects of his verse were not abstractions, dwelling apart in a glittering garment of words. They were the ordinary things which he saw round him, the birds and flowers of his orchard, the peasantry of his neighbourhood, the mendicants who came to his door. In this area there was little room for the play of fancy, and even those lyrics which he classified as 'poems of the fancy' are for the most part the fruit of the higher quality of imagination working, in lighter moments, upon subjects suggested by his immediate surroundings. Nothing was too common for him: the imagination found food in everything to which Nature lent life or interest. His subject was of primary importance to him: his aim was to describe it and what it meant to him directly and sincerely, without those flowers of phrase which may too easily become a covering for barrenness of thought. His style became the accurate reflexion of his subject. It rose and fell with it, and, where his choice rested, as it constantly did, upon things from which the commonplace element cannot be eliminated by any stretch of imagination, it faithfully reflected their prosaic aspect in lines which, like whole tracts of *The Excursion*, require considerable patience on the part of the reader to appreciate. The student of Wordsworth finds a difficulty in reconciling the apparent contradiction between passages of dulness and prolix meditation, the subjects of which hardly seem worth the time and trouble devoted to them, and those exalted moments in which, as Matthew Arnold said, ' Nature not only gave him the matter for his poem, but wrote his poem for him.' No poet can soar so high at times: none at times can touch so low a level. He can give ' light to the sun and music to the wind ' with a magic use of simple words which lift the heart and give endless scope to the imagination: on the other hand, he can plod along contentedly for line after line without affording or apparently feeling a single quickening impulse. The contrast is that which forms the main theme of *Intimations of Immortality*. The splendour of youthful visions has faded into ' the light of common day.' Much of Wordsworth's poetry necessarily reflects this, but with the compensation that from time to time the spark from heaven falls, and the quiet, unambitious verse is transfigured by

> The light that never was, on sea or land,
> The consecration, and the Poet's dream.

It should, however, be always kept in mind that, even where Wordsworth fails to do himself justice and appears to surrender himself willingly to tedium, he never loses sight of the importance of his poetic mission. He may exercise his office of teacher to excess: he may even enlarge upon a theme without illuminating it or he may philosophise upon the obvious; but his emotion is always sincere. The natural result is that those who put themselves under his guidance find more than appears at first sight in the studious quiet of his verse. Beneath its placid surface there is a reserve of feeling upon which the lover of poetry can always draw. His confidence in the faithfulness of Nature to those who will be led by her never fails: it is the influence which gives his poetry its supreme power of tranquilising and uplifting, of drawing aside the veil that hides from us 'to what fair countries we are bound.'

One particular district of England supplied Wordsworth with the most fruitful material for his verse. We speak of the 'Lake poets,' because Wordsworth lived at Grasmere, and Coleridge made his intermittent home for a few unhappy years at Keswick in the house permanently associated with the memory of Southey. But Coleridge is emphatically the poet, not of the Lake country, but of the Quantocks, amid which, in his native west, his most productive period was passed. The sources of Southey's poetry were his library, his love of early literature and romance. There is only one 'Lake poet' in the true sense of the term. Wordsworth was born upon the verge of the Lake country, where the Cocker, descending Lorton vale from Crummock water, falls into the Derwent. Nature revealed herself to him first on the surface of Esthwaite water and among the fells of Windermere and Coniston. His life at Racedown and Alfoxden had a profound influence upon his intellectual development; but the low hills and rich valleys of the west had little effect upon his powers of description. It has already been remarked that the interest of *Tintern Abbey* is its spiritual beauty: the actual scene, sketched in the most perfunctory manner, goes for nothing, save in so far as its peaceful charm prompted him to a retrospect of the long debt which he owed to Nature. In order to picture natural scenery completely, to give the spirit of Nature a local habitation and home, he needed the presence of lakes and mountains. Where his imagination rises to its full grandeur in *The Prelude*, it is among such scenes, in the silence of night upon Esthwaite, in the flying shadows and the brightness of sea and mountain when vows were made for him by Nature as the summer sun rose, in the disturbed solitude of the Grande Chartreuse beside the sister streams of Life and Death, amid the cliffs and torrents of Alpine passes, in the moonlit groves by the lake of Como, in the mountain mists through which the Cumbrian shepherd drives his flock, and on the slopes of Snowdon with the moon riding in the firmament and the hill-tops heaving their 'dusky backs' above the sea of fog below. The inspiration which makes these passages memorable comes from his native Lake country. Its barren mountain-summits, the tranquil sheets of water that lie securely within their folds, moulded his spirit into a form identical with their own. His mind became the mirror of their stern grandeur and their peace; and 'the voice of mountain-torrents' is audible again and again as we listen to his poetry, carrying far into our hearts ' a gentle shock of mild surprise.'

At the same time, just as poetic ornament is only a part, and not an indispensable part, of poetry, the power of describing scenery was only one aspect, and not the most essential aspect, of Wordsworth's debt to the Lakes. Nature did not confine herself to the task of infusing her personality into inanimate objects and giving them a being and a voice: her dwelling was everywhere,

> the light of setting suns,
> And the round ocean and the living air,
> And the blue sky, and in the mind of man.

The change of mind recorded in *Tintern Abbey* was wrought by the growing conviction, enforced upon Wordsworth during the most unsettled period of his life, of the abiding relationship between man and Nature. Nature was no mere external power, to be admired and feared: her spirit was inherent in man, bringing him into communion or possibility of communion with all that shared it, the influence which binds together the whole universe. To become the poet of Nature, Wordsworth had to emerge from solitary enjoyments into social life, to learn sympathy with his fellow-men. ' The still sad music of humanity ' taught him the true meaning of those early visitations which Nature had vouchsafed him. More especially, his experiences in France gave him a fellow-feeling for the poor and the oppressed. In their strife against hardships which threatened to overwhelm them, he found the virtues of independence, fortitude, mutual affection and self-sacrifice flourish most bravely. If an 'impulse from a vernal wood' can teach us more of man than all the sages, so the lessons of the unlettered and simple are of more value than the hoarded wisdom of book-learning. This is Wordsworth's constant theme in *Lyrical Ballads:* it is the substantive element which gives beauty and dignity to the unpretending verse of *Resolution and Independence* and *Ruth*, it is the quality which redeems *The Idiot Boy* and *Peter Bell* from the charge of wilful grotesqueness and intensifies the tragic pathos of *The Affliction of Margaret* and *The Thorn.* It called forth his highest lyrical gifts in *The Solitary Reaper* and in two only less beautiful poems of the Scottish tour of 1803, *To a Highland Girl* and *Stepping Westward.* Nowhere, however, did he find more opportunity for enlarging upon this subject than in the Lake country. The surroundings of Grasmere furnished him with the material of a pastoral life, led among difficulties and natural obstacles of a most formidable kind, shut out from the ordinary advantages of less sequestered districts, self-contained within the narrow bounds of arduous daily duty. Such a life might have provoked the gushings of a sentimentalist, content to admire and envy it for its merely artistic perfection. But Wordsworth loved and understood it, and lived among poor men with a kindred frugality. The Cumbrian peasant, farming his small plot of ground in daily conflict with the powers of Nature, became his type of the highest virtues, virtues which rose to meet the unremitting call of duty. Nature, the stern teacher and taskmistress, taught love as well as fear. The dangers of the mountains, mist, storm and precipice, were not merely risks against which the countryman had to guard. They became the inspiration of his life, forming his character, developing courage and self-reliance, and imbuing him with their own severity and nobility.

Wordsworth, contemplating the encouragement which he had derived from this source, found an analogy to his own case in the legend of the Shepherd lord, the heir of the house of Clifford, who, saved from the ruin of his family, learned the mercy and justice and tranquillity of soul unknown to his fathers among the shepherds of the valleys at the foot of Helvellyn. The calm stanzas which follow the ecstasies of the *Song at the Feast of Brougham Castle* apply to the romantic story the experience of Wordsworth himself:

> Love had he found in huts where poor men lie;
> His daily teachers had been woods and rills,
> The silence that is in the starry sky,
> The sleep that is among the lonely hills.

Of the active application of this training to the life and scenes which lay immediately round him, no more perfect illustration can be chosen than *Michael*. It is a narrative of the simplest kind, the story of a Grasmere cottager whose ambitions are centred upon the preservation of his small free-hold, maintained by toil in the face of difficulty which has become his second nature. His love for his only son, associated with all his labour, is bound up with the longing to transmit an unencumbered inheritance to him. The story is one of misfortune and disappointed hope: the heritage is threatened, the son is sent out into the world to earn money for its rescue, he forgets his father's parting adjurations and falls into evil courses, the old man is left to contemplate dispirited the unfinished sheepfold, the symbol of a broken covenant, and dies with his wishes unrealised. Wordsworth employs no ornament to decorate the story: it is told in the plainest terms, without any artificial attempt to heighten the pathos, but under the influence of a natural emotion which makes itself felt in every line. The greatest difficulty in expressing the characteristics of Wordsworth's poetry arises from the fact that they explain themselves so readily. He reflects his subject so directly and completely that insistence upon details becomes unnecessary. In this poem, of which the sheepfold of Greenhead Ghyll is the imaginative centre of an every-day drama, we have a complete picture in a small compass of the scenery and life which affected him most deeply—and not merely a picture, for the austerity of the verse blends itself inextricably with the rugged solitudes of its scene and the living figures which are at one with them. It springs directly from such life and scenery and, in so doing, communicates to them a permanent poetic form. Sincerity of emotion, the identity of the imagination with its object, could effect no greater triumph.

The emphasis which Wordsworth lays upon independence and self-reliance in such poems is one of the cardinal features of his verse. It has been shewn already that his quest of liberty found its ultimate haven in the freedom of the soul. The famous lines of *Laodamia*,

> Be taught, O faithful Consort, to control
> Rebellious passion: for the Gods approve
> The depth, and not the tumult, of the soul,

may be taken as the motto of his poetry, explaining and confirming its consistent quietism. At first sight, the point of view of his later life was the contradiction of his early enthusiasms. His revolutionary ardour gave place to submission to constituted authority. Younger men of letters, whose political thought was inspired by indignation at the restoration of the old French *régime* after the fall of Napoleon, regarded the conservatism of the so-called Lake poets as apostasy, and were not slow to satirise the contrast between their former republicanism and their present acceptance of government appointments. Southey, indeed, laid himself open to such attacks by his adulation of the throne in his laureate poems. Wordsworth, on the other hand, was guiltless of any direct denial of his early ideals. The intellectual history written at length in *The Prelude* gives a connected view of his progress through 'the tumult of the soul.' No one felt the ardour of the revolutionary period more profoundly or was more confident that France had reached the golden age by a short cut and destroyed the barriers of European liberty with a single effort. To one so convinced the sequel of the revolution was a bewildering calamity. Power which promised freedom revealed itself as new tyranny, and the golden age was as far off as ever. Wordsworth gradually came to recognise that beneath the surface of human action, with its baffling changes, lay permanent and stable forces, and that in the untroubled preception of these by the individual soul was the remedy for perplexity and disappointment. 'The One remains, the many change and pass.' From the contemplation of eternal being, unchangeable behind the mists raised by earthly passions, Wordsworth gained fortitude and hope and realised the freedom which Shelley celebrated in the victory of Prometheus over tyranny:

> To love, and bear; to hope till Hope creates
> From its own wreck the thing it contemplates;
> Neither to change, nor falter, nor repent.

To arrive, however, at this point of conviction, was not to be passionless or blind to the significance of outward events. If Wordsworth saw that obedience to duty was the securest road to freedom and, in following it, submitted to forms of which he had been impatient, he never lost sight of his enthusiasm for national liberty. His sense of loyalty to church, state and throne deepened with years and with the opening of an era of just and tolerant government, but it was a 'patriot loyalty' founded upon the assurance of the 'constancy inviolate' with which his nation had guided her destinies. While he stands supreme among his contemporaries as the lyric poet who best understood the message of Nature to man, none excelled him as the poet of national patriotism. His reverence for Milton pervades his verse: his blank verse instinctively took a Miltonic form and, in its constructions and turns of phrase constantly recalls its master, and the sonnets, those 'soul-animating strains' in which Milton spoke most directly of his passion for his country's liberty, incited him to imitation. Wordsworth obtained a command of the sonnet-form and its variations unexampled in English poetry, and used it to reflect all aspects of his thought. But his noblest sonnets are those in which he was stirred to the depths by the oppression or imminent danger of free nationalities. The fall of the Venetian republic, the conquest of Switzerland, the arming of the English nation to resist the threatened Napoleonic invasion, the inglorious concentration of his fellow-countrymen upon 'getting and spending,' gave occasion for strains of protest or encouragement fired with that enthusiasm for freedom which, from the days of the Athenian republic onwards, has been the kindling sentiment of the greatest epochs of literature. Wordsworth's patriotism was not confined within the limits of a single country or nation. Wherever he saw liberty striving to uphold her head, he gave his sympathy. But in the history of his own nation he recognised the most consistent and effective conflict in modern times against all that hinders the free development of the human spirit, and, while he freely condemned her backslidings, he as readily praised her manifestations of consciousness that she was 'sprung of Earth's first blood,' and welcomed, in her fidelity to her traditions, the surest guarantee of the greatness and freedom of the nations of the earth. Her story furnished him with the foremost examples of the ideal character which he described with energetic eloquence in *The Happy Warrior*, and the long sequence of *Ecclesiastical Sonnets*, which belong to the later period of his life and reflect its untroubled placidity and devotion to routine, has for its real subject, beneath the vicissitudes of the history of the national church, the growth of religious liberty in England.

Thus Wordsworth's place in the romantic movement is pre-eminently that of the interpreter of Nature to man, revealing her as the indwelling consoler and fortifier of the heart that is true to her lessons, teaching that the sincere emotion which is the gift her guidance brings is the source of that calm assurance which is the liberty of the soul. To claim that he, alone of the poets of his day, held the key to this secret would be too much. Coleridge shared it with him, but the versatility and impatience of his temperament were at war with the consistent use of it in his verse: he raises beautiful and surprising images before us, but they are the fragments of an incomplete and disconnected scheme of poetry, and his real grasp of poetic theory is discovered only in a few chapters of invaluable prose criticism. Wordsworth's verse communicated its meaning to Shelley, who again and again applies its teaching; but to Shelley the external accidents of shape and colour, which he described with unequalled beauty of phrase, were the veil, not the manifestation, of the inner form, tinged with its radiance, not permeated with its being. To Keats, on the other hand, the divinity of Nature was manifest, but each natural shape assumed its special godhead, as in antique mythology: Nature walked unveiled in manifold forms, and the one and indivisible presence that interfused all earthly objects was left unacknowledged. Between these extremes Wordsworth held the balance. His poetry is far less rich in dazzling effects: it is habitually bare, severe, unornamented. But its studious moderation of tone, avoiding all the pleasurable excitement of profuse colour and gorgeous epithet, yet pervaded by the deepest feeling, brings to its attentive reader the calm and hope of which, amid the discord of human life, we all stand in need. He is never aloof from humanity, building fabrics of visions: it is his poetic mission to be closely in touch with every-day life, to find his most profitable subjects in mankind. He is among that select band of poets from whom we may learn most readily 'to think clear, feel deep, bear fruit well'; and the moments, more frequent as we learn to know him better, at which, by virtue of his constant association of the visible object with the unseen power that gives dignity and beauty to the meanest things, his words ‘ trial clouds of glory ’ undimmed by contact with earth, communicate a personal happiness and sense of security to which poetry can afford few analogies.

REMEMBRANCE OF COLLINS

Composed upon the Thames near Richmond

Glide gently, thus for ever glide,
O Thames! that other bards may see
As lovely visions by thy side
As now, fair river! come to me.
O glide, fair stream! for ever so, 5
Thy quiet soul on all bestowing,
Till all our minds for ever flow
As thy deep waters now are flowing.

Vain thought!—Yet be as now thou art,
That in thy waters may be seen 10
The image of a poet's heart,
How bright, how solemn, how serene!
Such as did once the Poet bless,
Who, murmuring here a later ditty,
Could find no refuge from distress 15
But in the milder grief of pity.

Now let us, as we float along,
For *him* suspend the dashing oar;
And pray that never child of song
May know that Poet's sorrows more. 20

How calm! how still! the only sound,
The dripping of the oar suspended!
—The evening darkness gathers round
By virtue's holiest Powers attended.

EXPOSTULATION AND REPLY

'Why, William, on that old grey stone,
Thus for the length of half a day,
Why, William, sit you thus alone,
And dream your time away?

'Where are your books?—that light bequeathed 5
To Beings else forlorn and blind!
Up! up! and drink the spirit breathed
From dead men to their kind.

'You look round on your Mother Earth,
As if she for no purpose bore you; 10
As if you were her first-born birth,
And none had lived before you!'

One morning thus, by Esthwaite lake,
When life was sweet, I knew not why,
To me my good friend Matthew spake, 15
And thus I made reply:

'The eye—it cannot choose but see;
We cannot bid the ear be still;
Our bodies feel, where'er they be,
Against or with our will. 20

'Nor less I deem that there are Powers
Which of themselves our minds impress;
That we can feed this mind of ours
In a wise passiveness.

'Think you, 'mid all this mighty sum 25
Of things for ever speaking,
That nothing of itself will come,
But we must still be seeking?

'—Then ask not wherefore, here, alone,
Conversing as I may, 30
I sit upon this old grey stone,
And dream my time away.'

THE TABLES TURNED

An Evening Scene on the same Subject

Up! up! my Friend, and quit your books;
Or surely you'll grow double:
Up! up! my Friend, and clear your looks;
Why all this toil and trouble?

The sun, above the mountain's head, 5
A freshening lustre mellow
Through all the long green fields has spread,
His first sweet evening yellow.

Books! 'tis a dull and endless strife:
Come, hear the woodland linnet, 10
How sweet his music! on my life,
There's more of wisdom in it.

And hark! how blithe the throstle sings!
He, too, is no mean preacher:
Come forth into the light of things, 15
Let Nature be your Teacher.

She has a world of ready wealth,
Our minds and hearts to bless—
Spontaneous wisdom breathed by health,
Truth breathed by cheerfulness. 20

One impulse from a vernal wood
May teach you more of man,
Of moral evil and of good,
Than all the sages can.

Sweet is the lore which Nature brings; 25
Our meddling intellect
Mis-shapes the beauteous forms of things:—
We murder to dissect.

Enough of Science and of Art;
Close up those barren leaves; 30
Come forth, and bring with you a heart
That watches and receives.

TINTERN ABBEY

LINES COMPOSED A FEW MILES ABOVE TINTERN ABBEY, ON REVISITING THE BANKS OF THE WYE DURING A TOUR

July 13, 1798

Five years have past; five summers, with the length
Of five long winters! and again I hear
These waters, rolling from their mountain-springs
With a soft inland murmur.—Once again
Do I behold these steep and lofty cliffs, 5
That on a wild secluded scene impress
Thoughts of more deep seclusion; and connect
The landscape with the quiet of the sky.
The day is come when I again repose
Here, under this dark sycamore, and view 10
These plots of cottage-ground, these orchard-tufts,
Which at this season, with their unripe fruits,
Are clad in one green hue, and lose themselves
'Mid groves and copses. Once again I see
These hedge-rows, hardly hedge-rows, little lines 15
Of sportive wood run wild: these pastoral farms,
Green to the very door; and wreaths of smoke
Sent up, in silence, from among the trees!
With some uncertain notice, as might seem
Of vagrant dwellers in the houseless woods, 20

Or of some Hermit's cave, where by his fire
The Hermit sits alone.

These beauteous forms,
Through a long absence, have not been to me
As is a landscape to a blind man's eye:
But oft, in lonely rooms, and 'mid the din 25
Of towns and cities, I have owed to them,
In hours of weariness, sensations sweet
Felt in the blood, and felt along the heart;
And passing even into my purer mind,
With tranquil restoration:—feelings too 30
Of unremembered pleasure: such, perhaps,
As have no slight or trivial influence
On that best portion of a good man's life,
His little, nameless, unremembered acts
Of kindness and of love. Nor less, I trust, 35
To them I may have owed another gift,
Of aspect more sublime; that blessed mood,
In which the burthen of the mystery,
In which the heavy and the weary weight
Of all this unintelligible world, 40
Is lightened:—that serene and blessed mood,
In which the affections gently lead us on,—
Until, the breath of this corporeal frame
And even the motion of our human blood
Almost suspended, we are laid asleep 45
In body, and become a living soul:
While with an eye made quiet by the power

Of harmony, and the deep power of joy,
We see into the life of things.

If this
Be but a vain belief, yet, oh! how oft— 50
In darkness and amid the many shapes
Of joyless daylight; when the fretful stir
Unprofitable, and the fever of the world,
Have hung upon the beatings of my heart—
How oft, in spirit, have I turned to thee, 55
O sylvan Wye! thou wanderer thro' the woods,
How often has my spirit turned to thee!

And now, with gleams of half-extinguished thought,
With many recognitions dim and faint,
And somewhat of a sad perplexity, 60
The picture of the mind revives again:
While here I stand, not only with the sense
Of present pleasure, but with pleasing thoughts
That in this moment there is life and food
For future years. And so I dare to hope, 65
Though changed, no doubt, from what I was when first
I came among these hills; when like a roe
I bounded o'er the mountains, by the sides
Of the deep rivers, and the lonely streams,
Wherever Nature led: more like a man 70
Flying from something that he dreads, than one
Who sought the thing he loved. For Nature then
(The coarser pleasures of my boyish days,
And their glad animal movements all gone by)

To me was all in all.—I cannot paint 75
What then I was. The sounding cataract
Haunted me like a passion: the tall rock,
The mountain, and the deep and gloomy wood,
Their colours and their forms, were then to me
An appetite; a feeling and a love, 80
That had no need of a remoter charm,
By thought supplied, nor any interest
Unborrowed from the eye.—That time is past,
And all its aching joys are now no more,
And all its dizzy raptures. Not for this 85
Faint I, nor mourn nor murmur; other gifts
Have followed; for such loss, I would believe,
Abundant recompense. For I have learned
To look on Nature, not as in the hour
Of thoughtless youth; but hearing oftentimes 90
The still, sad music of humanity,
Nor harsh nor grating, though of ample power
To chasten and subdue. And I have felt
A presence that disturbs me with the joy
Of elevated thoughts; a sense sublime 95
Of something far more deeply interfused,
Whose dwelling is the light of setting suns,
And the round ocean, and the living air,
And the blue sky, and in the mind of man;
A motion and a spirit, that impels 100
All thinking things, all objects of all thought,
And rolls through all things. Therefore am I still
A lover of the meadows and the woods,

And mountains; and of all that we behold
From this green earth; of all the mighty world 105
Of eye, and ear,—both what they half create,
And what perceive; well pleased to recognise
In nature and the language of the sense
The anchor of my purest thoughts, the nurse,
The guide, the guardian of my heart, and soul 110
Of all my moral being.

Nor perchance,
If I were not thus taught, should I the more
Suffer my genial spirits to decay:
For thou art with me here upon the banks
Of this fair river; thou my dearest Friend, 115
My dear, dear Friend; and in thy voice I catch
The language of my former heart, and read
My former pleasures in the shooting lights
Of thy wild eyes. Oh! yet a little while
May I behold in thee what I was once, 120
My dear, dear Sister! and this prayer I make,
Knowing that Nature never did betray
The heart that loved her; 'tis her privilege,
Through all the years of this our life, to lead
From joy to joy: for she can so inform 125
The mind that is within us, so impress
With quietness and beauty, and so feed
With lofty thoughts, that neither evil tongues,
Rash judgments, nor the sneers of selfish men,
Nor greetings where no kindness is, nor all 130

The dreary intercourse of daily life,
Shall e'er prevail against us, or disturb
Our cheerful faith, that all which we behold
Is full of blessings. Therefore let the moon
Shine on thee in thy solitary walk; 135
And let the misty mountain-winds be free
To blow against thee: and, in after years,
When these wild ecstasies shall be matured
Into a sober pleasure; when thy mind
Shall be a mansion for all lovely forms, 140
Thy memory be as a dwelling-place
For all sweet sounds and harmonies; oh! then
If solitude, or fear, or pain, or grief,
Should be thy portion, with what healing thoughts
Of tender joy wilt thou remember me, 145
And these my exhortations! Nor, perchance—
If I should be where I no more can hear
Thy voice, nor catch from thy wild eyes these gleams
Of past existence—wilt thou then forget
That on the banks of this delightful stream 150
We stood together; and that I, so long
A worshipper of Nature, hither came
Unwearied in that service: rather say
With warmer love—oh! with far deeper zeal
Of holier love. Nor wilt thou then forget 155
That after many wanderings, many years
Of absence, these steep woods and lofty cliffs,
And this green pastoral landscape, were to me
More dear, both for themselves and for thy sake!

FROM PETER BELL

Long have I loved what I behold,
The night that calms, the day that cheers;
The common growth of mother-earth
Suffices me—her tears, her mirth,
Her humblest mirth and tears. 5

The dragon's wing, the magic ring,
I shall not covet for my dower,
If I along that lowly way
With sympathetic heart may stray,
And with a soul of power. 10

These given, what more need I desire
To stir, to soothe, or elevate?
What nobler marvels than the mind
May in life's daily prospect find,
May find or there create? 15

LUCY

Three years she grew in sun and shower,
Then Nature said, ' A lovelier flower
On earth was never sown;
This Child I to myself will take;
She shall be mine, and I will make 5
A Lady of my own.

' Myself will to my darling be
Both law and impulse: and with me

The Girl, in rock and plain,
In earth and heaven, in glade and bower, 10
Shall feel an overseeing power
To kindle or restrain.

'She shall be sportive as the fawn
That wild with glee across the lawn
Or up the mountain springs; 15
And hers shall be the breathing balm,
And hers the silence and the calm
Of mute insensate things.

'The floating clouds their state shall lend
To her; for her the willow bend; 20
Nor shall she fail to see
Even in the motions of the Storm
Grace that shall mould the Maiden's form
By silent sympathy.

'The stars of midnight shall be dear 25
To her; and she shall lean her ear
In many a secret place
Where rivulets dance their wayward round,
And beauty born of murmuring sound
Shall pass into her face. 30

'And vital feelings of delight
Shall rear her form to stately height,
Her virgin bosom swell;
Such thoughts to Lucy I will give
While she and I together live 35
Here in this happy dell.'

Thus Nature spake—The work was done—
How soon my Lucy's race was run!
She died, and left to me
This heath, this calm, and quiet scene; 40
The memory of what has been,
And never more will be.

SELECTIONS FROM MICHAEL

I. The Evening Star

Upon the forest-side in Grasmere Vale
There dwelt a Shepherd, Michael was his name;
An old man, stout of heart, and strong of limb.
His bodily frame had been from youth to age
Of an unusual strength: his mind was keen, 5
Intense, and frugal, apt for all affairs,
And in his shepherd's calling he was prompt
And watchful more than ordinary men.
Hence had he learned the meaning of all winds,
Of blasts of every tone; and oftentimes, 10
When others heeded not, He heard the South
Make subterraneous music, like the noise
Of bagpipers on distant Highland hills.
The Shepherd, at such warning, of his flock
Bethought him, and he to himself would say, 15
'The winds are now devising work for me!'
And, truly, at all times, the storm, that drives

The traveller to a shelter, summoned him
Up to the mountains: he had been alone
Amid the heart of many thousand mists, 20
That came to him, and left him, on the heights.
So lived he till his eightieth year was past.
And grossly that man errs, who should suppose
That the green valleys, and the streams and rocks,
Were things indifferent to the Shepherd's thoughts. 25
Fields, where with cheerful spirits he had breathed
The common air; hills, which with vigorous step
He had so often climbed; which had impressed
So many incidents upon his mind
Of hardship, skill or courage, joy or fear; 30
Which, like a book, preserved the memory
Of the dumb animals, whom he had saved,
Had fed or sheltered, linking to such acts
The certainty of honourable gain;
Those fields, those hills—what could they less? had
laid 35
Strong hold on his affections, were to him
A pleasurable feeling of blind love,
The pleasure which there is in life itself.

His days had not been passed in singleness.
His Helpmate was a comely matron, old— 40
Though younger than himself full twenty years.
She was a woman of a stirring life,
Whose heart was in her house: two wheels she had
Of antique form; this large, for spinning wool;

That small, for flax; and if one wheel had rest 45
It was because the other was at work.
The Pair had but one inmate in the house,
An only Child, who had been born to them
When Michael, telling o'er his years, began
To deem that he was old,—in shepherd's phrase, 50
With one foot in the grave. This only Son,
With two brave sheep-dogs tried in many a storm,
The one of an inestimable worth,
Made all their household. I may truly say,
That they were as a proverb in the vale 55
For endless industry. When day was gone,
And from their occupations out of doors
The Son and Father were come home, even then,
Their labour did not cease; unless when all
Turned to the cleanly supper-board, and there, 60
Each with a mess of pottage and skimmed milk,
Sat round the basket piled with oaten cakes,
And their plain home-made cheese. Yet when the meal
Was ended, Luke (for so the Son was named)
And his old Father both betook themselves 65
To such convenient work as might employ
Their hands by the fireside; perhaps to card
Wool for the Housewife's spindle, or repair
Some injury done to sickle, flail, or scythe,
Or other implement of house or field. 70

Down from the ceiling, by the chimney's edge,
That in our ancient uncouth country style

With huge and black projection overbrowed
Large space beneath, as duly as the light
Of day grew dim the Housewife hung a lamp; 75
An aged utensil, which had performed
Service beyond all others of its kind.
Early at evening did it burn—and late,
Surviving comrade of uncounted hours,
Which, going by from year to year, had found, 80
And left, the couple neither gay perhaps
Nor cheerful, yet with objects and with hopes,
Living a life of eager industry.
And now, when Luke had reached his eighteenth year,
There by the light of this old lamp they sate, 85
Father and Son, while far into the night
The Housewife plied her own peculiar work,
Making the cottage through the silent hours
Murmur as with the sound of summer flies.
This light was famous in its nieghbourhood, 90
And was a public symbol of the life
That thrifty Pair had lived. For, as it chanced,
Their cottage on a plot of rising ground
Stood single, with large prospect north and south,
High into Easedale, up to Dunmail-Raise, 95
And westward to the village near the lake;
And from this constant light, so regular,
And so far seen, the House itself, by all
Who dwelt within the limits of the vale,
Both old and young, was named THE EVENING STAR. 100

II. The Shepherd and his Son

But soon as Luke, full ten years old, could stand
Against the mountain blasts; and to the heights,
Not fearing toil, nor length of weary ways,
He with his Father daily went, and they
Were as companions, why should I relate 5
That objects which the Shepherd loved before
Were dearer now? that from the Boy there came
Feelings and emanations—things which were
Light to the sun and music to the wind;
And that the old Man's heart seemed born again? 10

III. The Unfinished Sheep-Fold

There is a comfort in the strength of love;
'Twill make a thing endurable, which else
Would overset the brain, or break the heart:
I have conversed with more than one who well
Remember the old Man, and what he was 5
Years after he had heard this heavy news.
His bodily frame had been from youth to age
Of an unusual strength. Among the rocks
He went, and still looked up to sun and cloud,
And listened to the wind; and, as before, 10
Performed all kinds of labour for his sheep,
And for the land, his small inheritance.
And to that hollow dell from time to time

Did he repair, to build the Fold of which
His flock had need. 'Tis not forgotten yet 15
The pity which was then in every heart
For the old Man—and 'tis believed by all
That many and many a day he thither went,
And never lifted up a single stone.

There, by the Sheep-fold, sometimes was he seen 20
Sitting alone, or with his faithful Dog,
Then old, beside him, lying at his feet.
The length of full seven years, from time to time,
He at the building of this Sheep-fold wrought,
And left the work unfinished when he died. 25
Three years, or little more, did Isabel
Survive her Husband: at her death the estate
Was sold, and went into a stranger's hand.
The Cottage which was named the EVENING STAR
Is gone—the ploughshare has been through the ground 30
On which it stood; great changes have been wrought
In all the neighbourhood:—yet the oak is left
That grew beside their door; and the remains
Of the unfinished Sheep-fold may be seen
Beside the boisterous brook of Greenhead Ghyll. 35

TO JOANNA

Amid the smoke of cities did you pass
The time of early youth; and there you learned,
From years of quiet industry, to love

The living Beings by your own fireside,
With such a strong devotion, that your heart 5
Is slow to meet the sympathies of them
Who look upon the hills with tenderness,
And make dear friendships with the streams and groves.
Yet we, who are transgressors in this kind,
Dwelling retired in our simplicity 10
Among the woods and fields, we love you well,
Joanna! and I guess, since you have been
So distant from us now for two long years,
That you will gladly listen to discourse,
However trivial, if you thence be taught 15
That they, with whom you once were happy, talk
Familiarly of you and of old times.

While I was seated, now some ten days past,
Beneath those lofty firs, that overtop
Their ancient neighbour, the old steeple-tower, 20
The Vicar from his gloomy house hard by
Came forth to greet me; and, when he had asked,
'How fares Joanna, that wild-hearted Maid,
And when will she return to us?' he paused;
And, after short exchange of village news, 25
He with grave looks demanded for what cause,
Reviving obsolete idolatry,
I, like a Runic Priest, in characters
Of formidable size had chiselled out
Some uncouth name upon the native rock, 30
Above the Rotha, by the forest-side.

—Now, by those dear immunities of heart
Engendered between malice and true love,
I was not loth to be so catechised,
And this was my reply:— ‘As it befell, 35
One summer morning we had walked abroad
At break of day, Joanna and myself.
—’Twas that delightful season when the broom,
Full-flowered, and visible on every steep,
Along the copses runs in veins of gold. 40
Our pathway led us on to Rotha’s banks;
And, when we came in front of that tall rock
That eastward looks, I there stopped short—and stood
Tracing the lofty barrier with my eye
From base to summit; such delight I found 45
To note in shrub and tree, in stone and flower,
That intermixture of delicious hues,
Along so vast a surface, all at once,
In one impression, by connecting force
Of their own beauty, imaged in the heart. 50
—When I had gazed perhaps two minutes’ space,
Joanna, looking in my eyes, beheld
That ravishment of mine, and laughed aloud.
The Rock, like something starting from a sleep,
Took up the Lady’s voice, and laughed again; 55
That ancient Woman seated on Helm-crag
Was ready with her cavern; Hammar-scar,
And the tall Steep of Silver-how, sent forth
A noise of laughter; southern Loughrigg heard,
And Fairfield answered with a mountain tone; 60

Helvellyn far into the clear blue sky
Carried the Lady's voice,—old Skiddaw blew
His speaking trumpet;—back out of the clouds
Of Glaramara southward came the voice;
And Kirkstone tossed it from his misty head. 65
—Now whether (said I to our cordial Friend,
Who in the hey-day of astonishment
Smiled in my face) this were in simple truth
A work accomplished by the brotherhood
Of ancient mountains, or my ear was touched 70
With dreams and visionary impulses
To me alone imparted, sure I am
That there was a loud uproar in the hills.
And, while we both were listening, to my side
The fair Joanna drew, as if she wished 75
To shelter from some object of her fear.
—And hence, long afterwards, when eighteen moons
Were wasted, as I chanced to walk alone
Beneath this rock, at sunrise, on a calm
And silent morning, I sat down, and there, 80
In memory of affections old and true,
I chiselled out in those rude characters
Joanna's name deep in the living stone:—
And I, and all who dwell by my fireside,
Have called the lovely rock, JOANNA'S ROCK.' 85

TO THE CUCKOO

O blithe New-comer! I have heard,
I hear thee and rejoice,
O Cuckoo! shall I call thee Bird,
Or but a wandering Voice?

While I am lying on the grass 5
Thy twofold shout I hear,
From hill to hill it seems to pass,
At once far off, and near.

Though babbling only to the Vale,
Of sunshine and of flowers, 10
Thou bringest unto me a tale
Of visionary hours.

Thrice welcome, darling of the Spring!
Even yet thou art to me
No bird, but an invisible thing, 15
A voice, a mystery;

The same whom in my school-boy days
I listened to; that Cry
Which made me look a thousand ways
In bush, and tree, and sky. 20

To seek thee did I often rove
Through woods and on the green;
And thou wert still a hope, a love;
Still longed for, never seen.

And I can listen to thee yet; 25
Can lie upon the plain
And listen, till I do beget
That golden time again.

O blessèd Bird! the earth we pace
Again appears to be 30
An unsubstantial, faery place;
That is fit home for thee!

MY HEART LEAPS UP WHEN I BEHOLD

My heart leaps up when I behold
  A rainbow in the sky:
So was it when my life began;
So is it now I am a man;
So be it when I shall grow old, 5
  Or let me die!
The Child is father of the Man;
And I could wish my days to be
Bound each to each by natural piety.

COMPOSED UPON WESTMINSTER BRIDGE
Sept. 3, 1802

Earth has not anything to show more fair:
Dull would he be of soul who could pass by
A sight so touching in its majesty:

This City now doth, like a garment, wear
The beauty of the morning; silent, bare, 5
Ships, towers, domes, theatres, and temples lie
Open unto the fields, and to the sky;
All bright and glittering in the smokeless air.
Never did sun more beautifully steep
In his first splendour, valley, rock, or hill; 10
Ne'er saw I, never felt, a calm so deep!
The river glideth at his own sweet will:
Dear God! the very houses seem asleep;
And all that mighty heart is lying still!

IT IS A BEAUTEOUS EVENING, CALM AND FREE

It is a beauteous evening, calm and free;
The holy time is quiet as a Nun
Breathless with adoration; the broad sun
Is sinking down in its tranquillity;
The gentleness of heaven broods o'er the Sea; 5
Listen! the mighty Being is awake,
And doth with his eternal motion make
A sound like thunder—everlastingly.
Dear Child! dear Girl! that walkest with me here,
If thou appear untouched by solemn thought 10
Thy nature is not therefore less divine:
Thou liest in Abraham's bosom all the year;
And worshipp'st at the Temple's inner shrine,
God being with thee when we know it not.

TO TOUSSAINT L'OUVERTURE

Toussaint, the most unhappy man of men!
Whether the whistling Rustic tend his plough
Within thy hearing, or thy head be now
Pillowed in some deep dungeon's earless den;—
O miserable Chieftain! where and when 5
Wilt thou find patience? Yet die not; do thou
Wear rather in thy bonds a cheerful brow:
Though fallen thyself, never to rise again,
Live, and take comfort. Thou hast left behind
Powers that will work for thee; air, earth, and skies; 10
There's not a breathing of the common wind
That will forget thee; thou hast great allies;
Thy friends are exultations, agonies,
And love, and man's unconquerable mind.

LONDON, 1802

Milton! thou shouldst be living at this hour:
England hath need of thee: she is a fen
Of stagnant waters: altar, sword, and pen,
Fireside, the heroic wealth of hall and bower,
Have forfeited their ancient English dower 5
Of inward happiness. We are selfish men;
Oh! raise us up, return to us again;
And give us manners, virtue, freedom, power.

Thy soul was like a Star, and dwelt apart;
Thou hadst a voice whose sound was like the sea: 10
Pure as the naked heavens, majestic, free,
So didst thou travel on life's common way,
In cheerful godliness; and yet thy heart
The lowliest duties on herself did lay.

COMPOSED AFTER A JOURNEY ACROSS THE HAMBLETON HILLS, YORKSHIRE

Dark and more dark the shades of evening fell;
The wished-for point was reached—but at an hour
When little could be gained from that rich dower
Of prospect, whereof many thousands tell.
Yet did the glowing west with marvellous power 5
Salute us; there stood Indian citadel,
Temple of Greece, and minster with its tower
Substantially expressed—a place for bell
Or clock to toll from! Many a tempting isle,
With groves that never were imagined, lay 10
'Mid seas how steadfast! objects all for the eye
Of silent rapture; but we felt the while
We should forget them; they are of the sky,
And from our earthly memory fade away.

TO THE DAISY

In youth from rock to rock I went,
From hill to hill in discontent
Of pleasure high and turbulent,
    Most pleased when most uneasy;
But now my own delights I make,— 5
My thirst at every rill can slake,
And gladly Nature's love partake
    Of thee, sweet Daisy!

Thee Winter in the garland wears
That thinly decks his few grey hairs; 10
Spring parts the clouds with softest airs,
    That she may sun thee;
Whole Summer-fields are thine by right;
And Autumn, melancholy Wight!
Doth in thy crimson head delight 15
    When rains are on thee.

In shoals and bands, a morrice train,
Thou greet'st the traveller in the lane;
Pleased at his greeting thee again;
    Yet nothing daunted, 20
Nor grieved if thou be set at nought:
And oft alone in nooks remote
We meet thee, like a pleasant thought,
    When such are wanted.

Be violets in their secret mews 25
The flowers the wanton Zephyrs choose;
Proud be the rose; with rains and dews
Her head impearling,
Thou liv'st with less ambitious aim,
Yet hast not gone without thy fame; 30
Thou art indeed by many a claim
The Poet's darling.

If to a rock from rains he fly,
Or, some bright day of April sky,
Imprisoned by hot sunshine lie 35
Near the green holly,
And wearily at length should fare;
He needs but look about, and there
Thou art!—a friend at hand, to scare
His melancholy. 40

A hundred times, by rock or bower,
Ere thus I have lain couched an hour,
Have I derived from thy sweet power
Some apprehension;
Some steady love; some brief delight; 45
Some memory that had taken flight;
Some chime of fancy wrong or right;
Or stray invention.

If stately passions in me burn,
And one chance look to thee should turn, 50
I drink out of an humbler urn
A lowlier pleasure;

The homely sympathy that heeds
The common life our nature breeds;
A wisdom fitted to the needs 55
    Of hearts at liesure.

Fresh-smitten by the morning ray,
When thou art up, alert and gay,
Then, cheerful Flower! my spirits play
    With kindred gladness: 60
And when, at dusk, by dews opprest
Thou sink'st, the image of thy rest
Hath often eased my pensive breast
    Of careful sadness.

And all day long I number yet, 65
All seasons through, another debt,
Which I, wherever thou art met,
    To thee am owing;
An instinct call it, a blind sense;
A happy, genial influence, 70
Coming one knows not how, nor whence,
    Nor whither going.

Child of the Year! that round dost run
Thy pleasant course,—when day's begun
As ready to salute the sun 75
    As lark or leveret,
Thy long-lost praise thou shalt regain;
Nor be less dear to future men
Than in old time;—thou not in vain
    Art Nature's favourite. 80

THE GREEN LINNET

Beneath these fruit-tree boughs that shed
Their snow-white blossoms on my head,
With brightest sunshine round me spread
    Of spring's unclouded weather,
In this sequestered nook how sweet 5
To sit upon my orchard-seat!
And birds and flowers once more to greet,
    My last year's friends together.

One have I marked, the happiest guest
In all this covert of the blest: 10
Hail to thee, far above the rest
    In joy of voice and pinion!
Thou, Linnet! in thy green array,
Presiding Spirit here to-day,
Dost lead the revels of the May; 15
    And this is thy dominion.

While birds, and butterflies, and flowers,
Make all one band of paramours,
Thou, ranging up and down the bowers,
    Art sole in thy employment: 20
A Life, a Presence like the Air,
Scattering thy gladness without care,
Too blest with any one to pair;
    Thyself thy own enjoyment.

Amid yon tuft of hazel trees, 25
That twinkle to the gusty breeze,
Behold him perched in ecstasies,
    Yet seeming still to hover;
There! where the flutter of his wings
Upon his back and body flings 30
Shadows and sunny glimmerings,
    That cover him all over.

My dazzled sight he oft deceives,
A Brother of the dancing leaves;
Then flits, and from the cottage eaves 35
    Pours forth his song in gushes;
As if by that exulting strain
He mocked and treated with disdain
The voiceless Form he chose to feign,
    While fluttering in the bushes. 40

YEW-TREES

There is a Yew-tree, pride of Lorton Vale,
Which to this day stands single, in the midst
Of its own darkness, as it stood of yore;
Not loth to furnish weapons for the bands
Of Umfraville or Percy ere they marched 5
To Scotland's heaths; or those that crossed the sea
And drew their sounding bows at Azincour,
Perhaps at earlier Crecy, or Poictiers.

Of vast circumference and gloom profound
This solitary Tree! a living thing 10
Produced too slowly ever to decay;
Of form and aspect too magnificent
To be destroyed. But worthier still of note
Are those fraternal Four of Borrowdale,
Joined in one solemn and capacious grove; 15
Huge trunks! and each particular trunk a growth
Of intertwisted fibres serpentine
Up-coiling, and inveterately convolved;
Nor uninformed with Phantasy, and looks
That threaten the profane; a pillared shade, 20
Upon whose grassless floor of red-brown hue,
By sheddings from the pining umbrage tinged
Perennially—beneath whose sable roof
Of boughs, as if for festal purpose decked
With unrejoicing berries—ghostly Shapes 25
May meet at noontide; Fear and trembling Hope,
Silence and Foresight; Death the Skeleton
And Time the Shadow;—there to celebrate,
As in a natural temple scattered o'er
With altars undisturbed of mossy stone, 30
United worship; or in mute repose
To lie, and listen to the mountain flood
Murmuring from Glaramara's inmost caves.

WHO FANCIED WHAT A PRETTY SIGHT

Who fancied what a pretty sight
This Rock would be if edged around
With living snow-drops? circlet bright!
How glorious to this orchard-ground!
Who loved the little Rock, and set 5
Upon its head this coronet?

Was it the humour of a child?
Or rather of some gentle maid,
Whose brows, the day that she was styled
The shepherd-queen, were thus arrayed? 10
Of man mature, or matron sage?
Or old man toying with his age?

I asked—'twas whispered; The device
To each and all might well belong:
It is the Spirit of Paradise 15
That prompts such work, a Spirit strong,
That gives to all the self-same bent
Where life is wise and innocent.

THE SOLITARY REAPER

Behold her, single in the field,
Yon solitary Highland Lass!
Reaping and singing by herself;
Stop here, or gently pass!

Alone she cuts and binds the grain, 5
And sings a melancholy strain;
O listen! for the Vale profound
Is overflowing with the sound.

No Nightingale did ever chaunt
More welcome notes to weary bands 10
Of travellers in some shady haunt
Among Arabian sands:
A voice so thrilling ne'er was heard
In spring-time from the Cuckoo-bird,
Breaking the silence of the seas 15
Among the farthest Hebrides.

Will no one tell me what she sings?—
Perhaps the plaintive numbers flow
For old, unhappy, far-off things,
And battles long ago: 20
Or is it some more humble lay,
Familiar matter of to-day?
Some natural sorrow, loss, or pain,
That has been, and may be again?

Whate'er the theme, the Maiden sang 25
As if her song could have no ending;
I saw her singing at her work,
And o'er the sickle bending;—
I listened, motionless and still;
And, as I mounted up the hill, 30
The music in my heart I bore,
Long after it was heard no more.

YARROW UNVISITED

From Stirling castle we had seen
The mazy Forth unravelled;
Had trod the banks of Clyde, and Tay,
And with the Tweed had travelled;
And when we came to Clovenford, 5
Then said my '*winsome Marrow*,'
'Whate'er betide, we'll turn aside,
And see the Braes of Yarrow.'

'Let Yarrow folk, *frae* Selkirk town,
Who have been buying, selling, 10
Go back to Yarrow, 'tis their own;
Each maiden to her dwelling!
On Yarrow's banks let herons feed,
Hares couch, and rabbits burrow!
But we will downward with the Tweed, 15
Nor turn aside to Yarrow.

'There's Galla Water, Leader Haughs,
Both lying right before us;
And Dryborough, where with chiming Tweed
The lintwhites sing in chorus; 20
There's pleasant Tiviot-dale, a land
Made blithe with plough and harrow:
Why throw away a needful day
To go in search of Yarrow?

'What's Yarrow but a river bare, 25
That glides the dark hills under?
There are a thousand such elsewhere
As worthy of your wonder.'
—Strange words they seemed of slight and scorn;
My True-love sighed for sorrow; 30
And looked me in the face, to think
I thus could speak of Yarrow!

'Oh! green,' said I, 'are Yarrow's holms,
And sweet is Yarrow flowing!
Fair hangs the apple frae the rock, 35
But we will leave it growing.
O'er hilly path, and open Strath,
We'll wander Scotland thorough;
But, though so near, we will not turn
Into the dale of Yarrow. 40

'Let beeves and home-bred kine partake
The sweets of Burn-mill meadow;
The swan on still St Mary's Lake
Float double, swan and shadow!
We will not see them; will not go, 45
To-day, nor yet to-morrow;
Enough if in our hearts we know
There's such a place as Yarrow.

'Be Yarrow stream unseen, unknown!
It must, or we shall rue it: 50
We have a vision of our own;
Ah! why should we undo it?

The treasured dreams of times long past,
We'll keep them, winsome Marrow!
For when we're there, although 'tis fair, 55
'Twill be another Yarrow!

' If Care with freezing years should come,
And wandering seem but folly,—
Should we be loth to stir from home,
And yet be melancholy; 60
Should life be dull, and spirits low,
'Twill soothe us in our sorrow,
That earth hath something yet to show,
The bonny holms of Yarrow!'

SHE WAS A PHANTOM OF DELIGHT

She was a Phantom of delight
When first she gleamed upon my sight;
A lovely Apparition, sent
To be a moment's ornament;
Her eyes as stars of Twilight fair; 5
Like Twilight's, too, her dusky hair;
But all things else about her drawn
From May-time and the cheerful Dawn;
A dancing Shape, an Image gay,
To haunt, to startle, and way-lay. 10

I saw her upon nearer view,
A Spirit, yet a Woman too!
Her household motions light and free,
And steps of virgin-liberty;
A countenance in which did meet 15
Sweet records, promises as sweet;
A Creature not too bright or good
For human nature's daily food;
For transient sorrows, simple wiles,
Praise, blame, love, kisses, tears, and smiles. 20

And now I see with eye serene
The very pulse of the machine;
A Being breathing thoughtful breath,
A Traveller between life and death;
The reason firm, the temperate will, 25
Endurance, foresight, strength, and skill;
A perfect Woman, nobly planned,
To warn, to comfort, and command;
And yet a Spirit still, and bright
With something of angelic light. 30

I WANDERED LONELY AS A CLOUD

I wandered lonely as a cloud
That floats on high o'er vales and hills,
When all at once I saw a crowd,
A host, of golden daffodils;
Beside the lake, beneath the trees, 5
Fluttering and dancing in the breeze.

Continuous as the stars that shine
And twinkle on the milky way,
They stretched in never-ending line
Along the margin of a bay: 10
Ten thousand saw I at a glance,
Tossing their heads in sprightly dance.

The waves beside them danced; but they
Out-did the sparkling waves in glee:
A poet could not but be gay, 15
In such a jocund company:
I gazed—and gazed—but little thought
What wealth the show to me had brought:

For oft, when on my couch I lie
In vacant or in pensive mood, 20
They flash upon that inward eye
Which is the bliss of solitude;
And then my heart with pleasure fills,
And dances with the daffodils.

ODE TO DUTY

Stern Daughter of the Voice of God!
O Duty! if that name thou love
Who art a light to guide, a rod
To check the erring, and reprove;
Thou, who art victory and law 5
When empty terrors overawe;

From vain temptations dost set free;
And calm'st the weary strife of frail humanity!

There are who ask not if thine eye
Be on them; who, in love and truth, 10
Where no misgiving is, rely
Upon the genial sense of youth:
Glad Hearts! without reproach or blot;
Who do thy work, and know it not:
Oh! if through confidence misplaced 15
They fail, thy saving arms, dread Power, around them
cast!

Serene will be our days and bright,
And happy will our nature be,
When love is an unerring light,
And joy its own security. 20
And they a blissful course may hold
Even now, who, not unwisely bold,
Live in the spirit of this creed;
Yet seek thy firm support, according to their need.

I, loving freedom, and untried; 25
No sport of every random gust,
Yet being to myself a guide,
Too blindly have reposed my trust:
And oft, when in my heart was heard
Thy timely mandate, I deferred 30
The task, in smoother walks to stray;
But thee I now would serve more strictly, if I may.

Through no disturbance of my soul,
Or strong compunction in me wrought,
I supplicate for thy control; 35
But in the quietness of thought:
Me this unchartered freedom tires;
I feel the weight of chance-desires:
My hopes no more must change their name,
I long for a repose that ever is the same. 40

Stern Lawgiver! yet thou dost wear
The Godhead's most benignant grace;
Nor know we anything so fair
As is the smile upon thy face:
Flowers laugh before thee on their beds 45
And fragrance in thy footing treads;
Thou dost preserve the stars from wrong;
And the most ancient Heavens, through thee, are
fresh and strong.

To humbler functions, awful Power!
I call thee: I myself commend 50
Unto thy guidance from this hour;
Oh, let my weakness have an end!
Give unto me, made lowly wise,
The spirit of self-sacrifice;
The confidence of reason give; 55
And in the light of truth thy Bondman let me live!

COMPOSED BY THE SIDE OF GRASMERE LAKE

Clouds, lingering yet, extend in solid bars
Through the grey west; and lo! these waters, steeled
By breezeless air to smoothest polish, yield
A vivid repetition of the stars;
Jove, Venus, and the ruddy crest of Mars 5
Amid his fellows beauteously revealed
At happy distance from earth's groaning field,
Where ruthless mortals wage incessant wars.
Is it a mirror?—or the nether Sphere
Opening to view the abyss in which she feeds 10
Her own calm fires?—But list! a voice is near;
Great Pan himself low-whispering through the reeds,
'Be thankful, thou; for, if unholy deeds
Ravage the world, tranquillity is here!'

WITH SHIPS THE SEA WAS SPRINKLED

With Ships the sea was sprinkled far and nigh,
Like stars in heaven, and joyously it showed;
Some lying fast at anchor in the road,
Some veering up and down, one knew not why.
A goodly vessel did I then espy 5
Come like a giant from a haven broad;
And lustily along the bay she strode,
Her tackling rich, and of apparel high.

The Ship was nought to me, nor I to her,
Yet I pursued her with a Lover's look; 10
This Ship to all the rest did I prefer:
When will she turn, and whither ? She will brook
No tarrying; where she comes the winds must stir:
On went she, and due north her journey took.

ODE

INTIMATIONS OF IMMORTALITY FROM RECOLLECTIONS OF EARLY CHILDHOOD

The Child is father of the Man;
And I could wish my days to be
Bound each to each by natural piety.

I.

There was a time when meadow, grove, and stream,
The earth, and every common sight,
To me did seem
Apparelled in celestial light,
The glory and the freshness of a dream. 5
It is not now as it hath been of yore;—
Turn wheresoe'er I may,
By night or day,
The things which I have seen I now can see no more.

II.

The Rainbow comes and goes, 10
And lovely is the Rose,
The Moon doth with delight
Look round her when the heavens are bare,
Waters on a starry night
Are beautiful and fair; 15
The sunshine is a glorious birth;
But yet I know, where'er I go,
That there hath passed away a glory from the earth.

III.

Now, while the birds thus sing a joyous song,
And while the young lambs bound 20
As to the tabor's sound,
To me alone there came a thought of grief:
A timely utterance gave that thought relief,
And I again am strong:
The cataracts blow their trumpets from the steep; 25
No more shall grief of mine the season wrong;
I hear the Echoes through the mountains throng,
The Winds come to me from the fields of sleep,
And all the earth is gay;
Land and sea 30
Give themselves up to jollity,
And with the heart of May
Doth every Beast keep holiday;—
Thou Child of Joy,
Shout round me, let me hear thy shouts, thou happy
Shepherd-boy! 35

IV.

Ye blessed Creatures, I have heard the call
Ye to each other make; I see
The heavens laugh with you in your jubilee;
My heart is at your festival,
My head hath its coronal, 40
The fulness of your bliss, I feel—I feel it all.
Oh evil day! if I were sullen
While Earth herself is adorning,
This sweet May-morning,
And the children are culling 45
On every side,
In a thousand valleys far and wide,
Fresh flowers; while the sun shines warm,
And the Babe leaps up on his Mother's arm:—
I hear, I hear, with joy I hear! 50
—But there's a Tree, of many, one,
A single Field which I have looked upon,
Both of them speak of something that is gone:
The Pansy at my feet
Doth the same tale repeat: 55
Whither is fled the visionary gleam?
Where is it now, the glory and the dream?

V.

Our birth is but a sleep and a forgetting:
The Soul that rises with us, our life's Star,
Hath had elsewhere its setting, 60
And cometh from afar:

Not in entire forgetfulness,
And not in utter nakedness,
But trailing clouds of glory do we come
From God, who is our home: 65
Heaven lies about us in our infancy!
Shades of the prison-house begin to close
Upon the growing Boy,
But He beholds the light, and whence it flows,
He sees it in his joy; 70
The Youth, who daily further from the east
Must travel, still is Nature's Priest,
And by the vision splendid
Is on his way attended;
At length the Man perceives it die away, 75
And fade into the light of common day.

VI.

Earth fills her lap with pleasures of her own;
Yearnings she hath in her own natural kind,
And, even with something of a Mother's mind,
And no unworthy aim, 80
The homely Nurse doth all she can
To make her Foster-child, her Inmate Man,
Forget the glories he hath known,
And that imperial palace whence he came.

VII.

Behold the Child among his new-born blisses, 85
A six years' Darling of a pigmy size!
See, where 'mid work of his own hand he lies,
Fretted by sallies of his mother's kisses,

With light upon him from his father's eyes!
See, at his feet, some little plan or chart, 90
Some fragment from his dream of human life,
Shaped by himself with newly-learned art;
A wedding or a festival,
A mourning or a funeral;
And this hath now his heart, 95
And unto this he frames his song:
Then will he fit his tongue
To dialogues of business, love, or strife;
But it will not be long
Ere this be thrown aside, 100
And with new joy and pride
The little Actor cons another part;
Filling from time to time his 'humorous stage'
With all the Persons, down to palsied Age,
That Life brings with her in her equipage; 105
As if his whole vocation
Were endless imitation.

VIII.

Thou, whose exterior semblance doth belie
Thy Soul's immensity;
Thou best philosopher, who yet dost keep 110
Thy heritage, thou Eye among the blind,
That, deaf and silent, read'st the eternal deep,
Haunted for ever by the eternal mind,—
Mighty Prophet! Seer blest!
On whom those truths do rest, 115

Which we are toiling all our lives to find,
In darkness lost, the darkness of the grave;
Thou, over whom thy Immortality
Broods like the Day, a Master o'er a Slave,
A Presence which is not to be put by; 120
Thou little Child, yet glorious in the might
Of heaven-born freedom on thy being's height,
Why with such earnest pains dost thou provoke
The years to bring the inevitable yoke,
Thus blindly with thy blessedness at strife? 125
Full soon thy Soul shall have her earthly freight,
And custom lie upon thee with a weight,
Heavy as frost, and deep almost as life!

IX.

O joy! that in our embers
Is something that doth live, 130
That nature yet remembers
What was so fugitive!
The thought of our past years in me doth breed
Perpetual benediction: not indeed
For that which is most worthy to be blest; 135
Delight and liberty, the simple creed
Of Childhood, whether busy or at rest,
With new-fledged hope still fluttering in his breast:—
Not for these I raise
The song of thanks and praise; 140

But for those obstinate questionings
Of sense and outward things,
Fallings from us, vanishings;
Blank misgivings of a Creature
Moving about in worlds not realised, 145
High instincts before which our mortal Nature
Did tremble like a guilty Thing surprised:
But for those first affections,
Those shadowy recollections,
Which, be they what they may, 150
Are yet the fountain-light of all our day,
Are yet a master-light of all our seeing;
Uphold us, cherish, and have power to make
Our noisy years seem moments in the being
Of the eternal Silence: truths that wake, 155
To perish never;
Which neither listlessness, nor mad endeavour,
Nor Man nor Boy,
Nor all that is at enmity with joy,
Can utterly abolish or destroy! 160
Hence in a season of calm weather
Though inland far we be,
Our Souls have sight of that immortal sea
Which brought us hither,
Can in a moment travel thither, 165
And see the Children sport upon the shore,
And hear the mighty waters rolling evermore.

X.

Then sing, ye Birds, sing, sing a joyous song!
    And let the young Lambs bound
    As to the tabor's sound! 170
We in thought will join your throng,
    Ye that pipe and ye that play,
    Ye that through your hearts to-day
    Feel the gladness of the May!
What though the radiance which was once so bright 175
Be now for ever taken from my sight,
    Though nothing can bring back the hour
Of splendour in the grass, of glory in the flower;
    We will grieve not, rather find
    Strength in what remains behind; 180
    In the primal sympathy
    Which having been must ever be;
    In the soothing thoughts that spring
    Out of human suffering;
    In the faith that looks through death, 185
In years that bring the philosophic mind.

XI.

And O, ye Fountains, Meadows, Hills, and Groves,
Forebode not any severing of our loves!
Yet in my heart of hearts I feel your might;
I only have relinquished one delight 190
To live beneath your more habitual sway.
I love the Brooks which down their channels fret,

Even more than when I tripped lightly as they;
The innocent brightness of a new-born Day
Is lovely yet; 195
The Clouds that gather round the setting sun
Do take a sober colouring from an eye
That hath kept watch o'er man's mortality;
Another race hath been, and other palms are won.
Thanks to the human heart by which we live, 200
Thanks to its tenderness, its joys, and fears,
To me the meanest flower that blows can give
Thoughts that do often lie too deep for tears.

THOUGHT OF A BRITON ON THE SUBJUGATION OF SWITZERLAND

Two Voices are there; one is of the sea,
One of the mountains; each a mighty Voice:
In both from age to age thou didst rejoice,
They were thy chosen music, Liberty!
There came a Tyrant, and with holy glee 5
Thou fought'st against him, but hast vainly striven:
Thou from thy Alpine holds at length art driven,
Where not a torrent murmurs heard by thee.
Of one deep bliss thine ear hath been bereft:
Then cleave, O cleave to that which still is left; 10
For, high-souled Maid, what sorrow would it be
That Mountain floods should thunder as before,
And Ocean bellow from his rocky shore,
And neither awful voice be heard by thee!

SONG AT THE FEAST OF BROUGHAM CASTLE,

UPON THE RESTORATION OF LORD CLIFFORD, THE SHEPHERD, TO THE ESTATES AND HONOURS OF HIS ANCESTORS

High in the breathless Hall the Minstrel sate,
And Emont's murmur mingled with the Song.—
The words of ancient time I thus translate,
A festal strain that hath been silent long:—

‘ From town to town, from tower to tower, 5
The red rose is a gladsome flower.
Her thirty years of winter past,
The red rose is revived at last;
She lifts her head for endless spring,
For everlasting blossoming: 10
Both roses flourish, red and white:
In love and sisterly delight
The two that were at strife are blended,
And all old troubles now are ended.—
Joy! joy to both! but most to her 15
Who is the flower of Lancaster!
Behold her how she smiles to-day
On this great throng, this bright array!
Fair greeting doth she send to all
From every corner of the hall; 20

But chiefly from above the board
Where sits in state our rightful Lord,
A Clifford to his own restored!

'They came with banner, spear, and shield,
And it was proved in Bosworth-field. 25
Not long the Avenger was withstood—
Earth helped him with the cry of blood:
St George was for us, and the might
Of blessed Angels crowned the right.
Loud voice the Land has uttered forth, 30
We loudest in the faithful north:
Our fields rejoice, our mountains ring,
Our streams proclaim a welcoming;
Our strong-abodes and castles see
The glory of their loyalty. 35

'How glad is Skipton at this hour—
Though lonely, a deserted Tower;
Knight, squire, and yeoman, page and groom;
We have them at the feast of Brough'm.
How glad Pendragon—though the sleep 40
Of years be on her!—She shall reap
A taste of this great pleasure, viewing
As in a dream her own renewing.
Rejoiced is Brough, right glad, I deem,
Beside her little humble stream; 45
And she that keepeth watch and ward
Her statelier Eden's course to guard;

They both are happy at this hour,
Though each is but a lonely Tower:—
But here is perfect joy and pride 50
For one fair House by Emont's side,
This day, distinguished without peer
To see her Master and to cheer—
Him and his Lady-mother dear!

'Oh! it was a time forlorn 55
When the fatherless was born—
Give her wings that she may fly,
Or she sees her infant die!
Swords that are with slaughter wild
Hunt the Mother and the Child. 60
Who will take them from the light?
—Yonder is a man in sight—
Yonder is a house—but where?
No, they must not enter there.
To the caves, and to the brooks, 65
To the clouds of heaven she looks;
She is speechless, but her eyes
Pray in ghostly agonies.
Blissful Mary, Mother mild,
Maid and Mother undefiled, 70
Save a Mother and her Child!

'Now who is he that bounds with joy
On Carrock's side, a Shepherd-boy?
No thoughts hath he but thoughts that pass
Light as the wind along the grass. 75

Can this be he who hither came
In secret, like a smothered flame?
O'er whom such thankful tears were shed
For shelter, and a poor man's bread!
God loves the Child; and God hath willed 80
That those dear words should be fulfilled,
The Lady's words, when forced away,
The last she to her Babe did say:
" My own, my own, thy Fellow-guest
I may not be; but rest thee, rest, 85
For lowly shepherd's life is best!"

' Alas! when evil men are strong
No life is good, no pleasure long.
The Boy must part from Mosedale's groves,
And leave Blencathara's rugged coves, 90
And quit the flowers that summer brings
To Glenderamakin's lofty springs;
Must vanish, and his careless cheer
Be turned to heaviness and fear.
—Give Sir Lancelot Threlkeld praise! 95
Hear it, good man, old in days!
Thou tree of covert and of rest
For the young Bird that is distrest;
Among thy branches safe he lay,
And he was free to sport and play, 100
When falcons were abroad for prey.

' A recreant harp, that sings of fear
And heaviness in Clifford's ear!

I said, when evil men are strong,
No life is good, no pleasure long, 105
A weak and cowardly untruth!
Our Clifford was a happy Youth,
And thankful through a weary time,
That brought him up to manhood's prime.
—Again he wanders forth at will, 110
And tends a flock from hill to hill:
His garb is humble; ne'er was seen
Such garb with such a noble mien;
Among the shepherd-grooms no mate
Hath he, a Child of strength and state! 115
Yet lacks not friends for simple glee,
Nor yet for higher sympathy.
To his side the fallow-deer
Came, and rested without fear;
The eagle, lord of land and sea, 120
Stooped down to pay him fealty;
And both the undying fish that swim
Through Bowscale-tarn did wait on him;
The pair were servants of his eye
In their immortality; 125
And glancing, gleaming, dark or bright,
Moved to and fro, for his delight.
He knew the rocks which Angels haunt
Upon the mountains visitant;
He hath kenned them taking wing: 130
And into caves where Faeries sing
He hath entered; and been told

By Voices how men lived of old.
Among the heavens his eye can see
The face of thing that is to be; 135
And, if that men report him right,
His tongue could whisper words of might.
—Now another day is come,
Fitter hope, and nobler doom;
He hath thrown aside his crook, 140
And hath buried deep his book;
Armour rusting in his halls
On the blood of Clifford calls;—
" Quell the Scot," exclaims the Lance—
Bear me to the heart of France, 145
Is the longing of the Shield—
Tell thy name, thou trembling Field;
Field of death, where'er thou be,
Groan thou with our victory!
Happy day, and mighty hour, 150
When our Shepherd, in his power,
Mailed and horsed, with lance and sword,
To his ancestors restored
Like a re-appearing Star,
Like a glory from afar, 155
First shall head the flock of war!'

Alas! the impassioned minstrel did not know
How, by Heaven's grace, this Clifford's heart was framed:
How he, long forced in humble walks to go,
Was softened into feeling, soothed, and tamed. 160

Love had he found in huts where poor men lie;
His daily teachers had been woods and rills,
The silence that is in the starry sky,
The sleep that is among the lonely hills.

In him the savage virtue of the Race, 165
Revenge, and all ferocious thoughts were dead:
Nor did he change; but kept in lofty place
The wisdom which adversity had bred.

Glad were the vales, and every cottage hearth;
The Shepherd-lord was honoured more and more; 170
And, ages after he was laid in earth,
'The good Lord Clifford' was the name he bore.

GEORGE AND SARAH GREEN

Who weeps for strangers? Many wept
  For George and Sarah Green;
Wept for that pair's unhappy fate,
  Whose grave may here be seen.

By night, upon these stormy fells, 5
  Did wife and husband roam;
Six little ones at home had left,
  And could not find that home.

For *any* dwelling-place of man
  As vainly did they seek. 10
He perished; and a voice was heard—
  The widow's lonely shriek.

Not many steps, and she was left
  A body without life—
A few short steps were the chain that bound 15
  The husband to the wife.

Now do those sternly-featured hills
  Look gently on this grave;
And quiet *now* are the depths of air,
  As a sea without a wave. 20

But deeper lies the heart of peace
  In quiet more profound;
The heart of quietness is here
  Within this churchyard bound.

And from all agony of mind 25
  It keeps them safe, and far
From fear and grief, and from all need
  Of sun or guiding star.

O darkness of the grave! how deep,
  After that living night— 30
That last and dreary living one
  Of sorrow and affright!

O sacred marriage-bed of death,
  That keeps them side by side
In bond of peace, in bond of love, 35
  They may not be untied!

YARROW VISITED

And is this—Yarrow?—*This* the Stream
Of which my fancy cherished,
So faithfully, a waking dream?
An image that hath perished!
O that some Minstrel's harp were near, 5
To utter notes of gladness,
And chase this silence from the air,
That fills my heart with sadness!

Yet why?—a silvery current flows
With uncontrolled meanderings; 10
Nor have these eyes by greener hills
Been soothed, in all my wanderings.
And through her depths, Saint Mary's Lake
Is visibly delighted;
For not a feature of those hills 15
Is in the mirror slighted.

A blue sky bends o'er Yarrow Vale,
Save where that pearly whiteness
Is round the rising sun diffused,
A tender hazy brightness; 20
Mild dawn of promise! that excludes
All profitless dejection;
Though not unwilling here to admit
A pensive recollection.

Where was it that the famous Flower 25
Of Yarrow Vale lay bleeding?
His bed perchance was yon smooth mound
On which the herd is feeding:
And haply from this crystal pool,
Now peaceful as the morning, 30
The Water-wraith ascended thrice—
And gave his doleful warning.
Delicious is the Lay that sings
The haunts of happy Lovers,
The path that leads them to the grove, 35
The leafy grove that covers:
And Pity sanctifies the Verse
That paints, by strength of sorrow,
The unconquerable strength of love;
Bear witness, rueful Yarrow! 40

But thou, that didst appear so fair
To fond imagination,
Dost rival in the light of day
Her delicate creation:
Meek loveliness is round thee spread, 45
A softness still and holy;
The grace of forest charms decayed,
And pastoral melancholy.

That region left, the vale unfolds
Rich groves of lofty stature, 50
With Yarrow winding through the pomp
Of cultivated nature;

And, rising from those lofty groves,
Behold a Ruin hoary!
The shattered front of Newark's Towers, 55
Renowned in Border story.

Fair scenes for childhood's opening bloom,
For sportive youth to stray in;
For manhood to enjoy his strength;
And age to wear away in! 60
Yon cottage seems a bower of bliss,
A covert for protection
Of tender thoughts, that nestle there—
The brood of chaste affection.

How sweet, on this autumnal day, 65
The wild-wood fruits to gather,
And on my True-love's forehead plant
A crest of blooming heather!
And what if I enwreathed my own!
'Twere no offence to reason; 70
The sober Hills thus deck their brows
To meet the wintry season.

I see—but not by sight alone,
Loved Yarrow, have I won thee;
A ray of fancy still survives— 75
Her sunshine plays upon thee!
Thy ever-youthful waters keep
A course of lively pleasure;
And gladsome notes my lips can breathe,
Accordant to the measure. 80

The vapours linger round the Heights,
They melt, and soon must vanish;
One hour is theirs, nor more is mine—
Sad thought, which I would banish,
But that I know, where'er I go, 85
Thy genuine image, Yarrow!
Will dwell with me—to heighten joy,
And cheer my mind in sorrow.

COMPOSED UPON AN EVENING OF EXTRAORDINARY SPLENDOUR AND BEAUTY

I.

Had this effulgence disappeared
With flying haste, I might have sent,
Among the speechless clouds, a look
Of blank astonishment;
But 'tis endued with power to stay, 5
And sanctify one closing day,
That frail Mortality may see—
What is?—ah no, but what *can* be!
Time was when field and watery cove
With modulated echoes rang, 10
While choirs of fervent Angels sang
Their vespers in the grove;
Or, crowning, star-like, each some sovereign height,
Warbled, for heaven above and earth below,

Strains suitable to both.—Such holy rite, 15
Methinks, if audibly repeated now
From hill or valley, could not move
Sublimer transport, purer love,
Than doth this silent spectacle—the gleam—
The shadow—and the peace supreme! 20

II.

No sound is uttered,—but a deep
And solemn harmony pervades
The hollow vale from steep to steep,
And penetrates the glades.
Far-distant images draw nigh, 25
Called forth by wondrous potency
Of beamy radiance, that imbues
Whate'er it strikes with gem-like hues!
In vision exquisitely clear,
Herds range along the mountain side; 30
And glistening antlers are descried;
And gilded flocks appear.
Thine is the tranquil hour, purpureal Eve!
But long as god-like wish, or hope divine,
Informs my spirit, ne'er can I believe 35
That this magnificence is wholly thine!
—From worlds not quickened by the sun
A portion of the gift is won;
An intermingling of Heaven's pomp is spread
On ground which British shepherds tread! 40

III.

And if there be whom broken ties
Afflict, or injuries assail,
Yon hazy ridges to their eyes
Present a glorious scale,
Climbing suffused with sunny air, 45
To stop—no record hath told where!
And tempting Fancy to ascend,
And with immortal Spirits blend!
—Wings at my shoulders seem to play;
But, rooted here, I stand and gaze 50
On those bright steps that heavenward raise
Their practicable way.
Come forth, ye drooping old men, look abroad,
And see to what fair countries ye are bound!
And if some traveller, weary of his road, 55
Hath slept since noon-tide on the grassy ground,
Ye Genii! to his covert speed;
And wake him with such gentle heed
As may attune his soul to meet the dower
Bestowed on this transcendent hour! 60

IV.

Such hues from their celestial Urn
Were wont to stream before mine eye,
Where'er it wandered in the morn
Of blissful infancy.
This glimpse of glory, why renewed? 65

Nay, rather speak with gratitude;
For, if a vestige of those gleams
Survived, 'twas only in my dreams.
Dread Power! whom peace and calmness serve
No less than Nature's threatening voice, 70
If aught unworthy be my choice,
From THEE if I would swerve,
Oh, let Thy grace remind me of the light
Full early lost, and fruitlessly deplored;
Which, at this moment, on my waking sight 75
Appears to shine, by miracle restored;
My soul, though yet confined to earth,
Rejoices in a second birth!
—'Tis past, the visionary splendour fades;
And night approaches with her shades. 80

WRITTEN UPON A BLANK LEAF IN 'THE COMPLETE ANGLER'

While flowing rivers yield a blameless sport,
Shall live the name of Walton: Sage benign!
Whose pen, the mysteries of the rod and line
Unfolding, did not fruitlessly exhort
To reverend watching of each still report 5
That Nature utters from her rural shrine.
Meek, nobly versed in simple discipline,
He found the longest summer day too short,

To his loved pastime given by sedgy Lee,
Or down the tempting maze of Shawford brook— 10
Fairer than life itself, in this sweet Book,
The cowslip-bank and shady willow-tree;
And the fresh meads—where flowed, from every nook
Of his full bosom, gladsome Piety!

TO THE REV. DR WORDSWORTH

The Minstrels played their Christmas tune
To-night beneath my cottage-eaves;
While, smitten by a lofty moon,
The encircling laurels, thick with leaves,
Gave back a rich and dazzling sheen, 5
That overpowered their natural green.

Through hill and valley every breeze
Had sunk to rest with folded wings:
Keen was the air, but could not freeze,
Nor check, the music of the strings; 10
So stout and hardy were the band
That scraped the chords with strenuous hand!

And who but listened?—till was paid
Respect to every Inmate's claim:
The greeting given, the music played, 15
In honour of each household name,
Duly pronounced with lusty call,
And 'Merry Christmas' wished to all.

O Brother! I revere the choice
That took thee from thy native hills; 20
And it is given thee to rejoice:
Though public care full often tills
(Heaven only witness of the toil)
A barren and ungrateful soil.

Yet, would that thou, with me and mine, 25
Hadst heard this never-failing rite;
And seen on other faces shine
A true revival of the light
Which Nature and these rustic Powers,
In simple childhood, spread through ours! 30

For pleasure hath not ceased to wait
On these expected annual rounds;
Whether the rich man's sumptuous gate
Call forth the unelaborate sounds,
Or they are offered at the door 35
That guards the lowliest of the poor.

How touching, when, at midnight, sweep
Snow-muffled winds, and all is dark,
To hear—and sink again to sleep!
Or, at an earlier call, to mark, 40
By blazing fire, the still suspense
Of self-complacent innocence;

The mutual nod,—the grave disguise
Of hearts with gladness brimming o'er;
And some unbidden tears that rise 45
For names once heard, and heard no more;

Tears brightened by the serenade
For infant in the cradle laid.

Ah! not for emerald fields alone,
With ambient streams more pure and bright 50
Than fabled Cytherea's zone
Glittering before the Thunderer's sight,
Is to my heart of hearts endeared
The ground where we were born and reared!

Hail, ancient Manners! sure defence, 55
Where they survive, of wholesome laws;
Remnants of love whose modest sense
Thus into narrow room withdraws;
Hail, Usages of pristine Mould,
And ye that guard them, Mountains old! 60

Bear with me, Brother! quench the thought
That slights this passion, or condemns;
If thee fond Fancy ever brought
From the proud margin of the Thames,
And Lambeth's venerable towers, 65
To humbler streams, and greener bowers.

Yes, they can make, who fail to find,
Short leisure even in busiest days;
Moments, to cast a look behind,
And profit by those kindly rays 70
That through the clouds do sometimes steal,
And all the far-off past reveal.

Hence, while the imperial City's din
Beats frequent on the satiate ear,
A pleased attention I may win 75
To agitations less severe,
That neither overwhelm nor cloy,
But fill the hollow vale with joy!

FROM THE RIVER DUDDON

V.

Sole listener, Duddon! to the breeze that played
With thy clear voice, I caught the fitful sound
Wafted o'er sullen moss and craggy mound—
Unfruitful solitudes, that seemed to upbraid
The sun in heaven!—but now, to form a shade 5
For thee, green alders have together wound
Their foliage; ashes flung their arms around;
And birch-trees risen in silver colonnade.
And thou hast also tempted here to rise,
'Mid sheltering pines, this Cottage rude and grey; 10
Whose ruddy children, by the mother's eyes
Carelessly watched, sport through the summer day,
Thy pleased associates:—light as endless May
On infant bosoms lonely Nature lies.

XXI.

Whence that low voice?—A whisper from the heart.
That told of days long past, when here I roved

With friends and kindred tenderly beloved;
Some who had early mandates to depart,
Yet are allowed to steal my path athwart 5
By Duddon's side; once more do we unite,
Once more, beneath the kind Earth's tranquil light;
And smothered joys into new being start.
From her unworthy seat, the cloudy stall
Of Time, breaks forth triumphant Memory; 10
Her glistening tresses bound, yet light and free
As golden locks of birch, that rise and fall
On gales that breathe too gently to recall
Aught of the fading year's inclemency!

XXVI.

Return, Content! for fondly I pursued,
Even when a child, the Streams—unheard, unseen;
Through tangled woods, impending rocks between;
Or, free as air, with flying inquest viewed
The sullen reservoirs whence their bold brood— 5
Pure as the morning, fretful, boisterous, keen,
Green as the salt-sea billows, white and green—
Poured down the hills, a choral multitude!
Nor have I tracked their course for scanty gains;
They taught me random cares and truant joys, 10
That shield from mischief and preserve from stains
Vague minds, while men are growing out of boys;
Maturer Fancy owes to their rough noise
Impetuous thoughts that brook not servile reins.

XXXIV.

AFTER-THOUGHT

I thought of thee, my partner and my guide,
As being past away.—Vain sympathies!
For backward, Duddon! as I cast my eyes,
I see what was, and is, and will abide;
Still glides the Stream, and shall for ever glide; 5
The Form remains, the Function never dies;
While we, the brave, the mighty, and the wise,
We men, who in our morn of youth defied
The elements, must vanish;—be it so!
Enough, if something from our hands have power 10
To live, and act, and serve the future hour;
And if, as toward the silent tomb we go,
Through love, through hope, and faith's transcendent
dower,
We feel that we are greater than we know.

HYMN

FOR THE BOATMEN, AS THEY APPROACH THE RAPIDS UNDER THE CASTLE OF HEIDELBERG

Jesu! bless our slender Boat,
By the current swept along;
Loud its threatenings—let them not
Drown the music of a song
Breathed thy mercy to implore, 5
Where these troubled waters roar!

Saviour, for our warning, seen
    Bleeding on that precious Rood;
If, while through the meadows green
    Gently wound the peaceful flood, 10
We forgot Thee, do not Thou
Disregard thy Suppliants now!

Hither, like yon ancient Tower
    Watching o'er the River's bed,
Fling the shadow of thy power, 15
    Else we sleep among the dead;
Thou who trod'st the billowy sea,
Shield us in our jeopardy!

Guide our Bark among the waves;
    Through the rocks our passage smooth; 20
Where the whirlpool frets and raves
    Let thy love its anger soothe:
All our hope is placed in Thee;
Miserere Domine!

THE SOURCE OF THE DANUBE

Not, like his great Compeers, indignantly
Doth DANUBE spring to life! The wandering Stream
(Who loves the Cross, yet to the Crescent's gleam
Unfolds a willing breast) with infant glee
Slips from his prison walls: and Fancy, free 5
To follow in his track of silver light,
Mounts on rapt wing, and with a moment's flight

Hath reached the encincture of that gloomy sea
Whose waves the Orphean lyre forbade to meet
In conflict; whose rough winds forgot their jars 10
To waft the heroic progeny of Greece;
When the first Ship sailed for the Golden Fleece—
ARGO—exalted for that daring feat
To fix in heaven her shape distinct with stars.

COMPOSED IN ONE OF THE CATHOLIC CANTONS

Doomed as we are our native dust
To wet with many a bitter shower,
It ill befits us to disdain
The altar, to deride the fane,
Where simple Sufferers bend, in trust 5
To win a happier hour.

I love, where spreads the village lawn,
Upon some knee-worn cell to gaze:
Hail to the firm, unmoving cross,
Aloft, where pines their branches toss! 10
And to the chapel far withdrawn,
That lurks by lonely ways!

Where'er we roam—along the brink
Of Rhine—or by the sweeping Po,
Through Alpine vale, or champaign wide, 15
Whate'er we look on, at our side
Be Charity!—to bid us think,
And feel, if we would know.

WALTON'S BOOK OF LIVES

There are no colours in the fairest sky
So fair as these. The feather, whence the pen
Was shaped that traced the lives of these good men,
Dropped from an Angel's wing. With moistened eye
We read of faith and purest charity 5
In Statesman, Priest, and humble Citizen:
Oh could we copy their mild virtues, then
What joy to live, what blessedness to die!
Methinks their very names shine still and bright;
Apart—like glow-worms on a summer night; 10
Or lonely tapers when from far they fling
A guiding ray; or seen—like stars on high,
Satellites burning in a lucid ring
Around meek Walton's heavenly memory.

SCORN NOT THE SONNET

Scorn not the Sonnet; Critic, you have frowned
Mindless of its just honours; with this key
Shakespeare unlocked his heart; the melody
Of this small lute gave ease to Petrarch's wound;
A thousand times this pipe did Tasso sound; 5
With it Camoëns soothed an exile's grief;
The Sonnet glittered a gay myrtle leaf
Amid the cypress with which Dante crowned

His visionary brow; a glow-worm lamp,
It cheered mild Spenser, called from Faery-land 10
To struggle through dark ways; and, when a damp
Fell round the path of Milton, in his hand
The Thing became a trumpet; whence he blew
Soul-animating strains—alas, too few!

GLAD SIGHT WHEREVER NEW WITH OLD

Glad sight wherever new with old
Is joined through some dear homeborn tie;
The life of all that we behold
Depends upon that mystery.
Vain is the glory of the sky, 5
The beauty vain of field and grove,
Unless, while with admiring eye
We gaze, we also learn to love.

THE UNREMITTING VOICE OF NIGHTLY STREAMS

The unremitting voice of nightly streams
That wastes so oft, we think, its tuneful powers,
If neither soothing to the worm that gleams
Through dewy grass, nor small birds hushed in bowers,
Nor unto silent leaves and drowsy flowers,— 5
That voice of unpretending harmony
(For who what is shall measure by what seems

To be, or not to be,
Or tax high Heaven with prodigality?)
Wants not a healing influence that can creep 10
Into the human breast, and mix with sleep
To regulate the motion of our dreams
For kindly issues—as through every clime
Was felt near murmuring brooks in earliest time;
As, at this day, the rudest swains who dwell 15
Where torrents roar, or hear the tinkling knell
Of water-breaks, with grateful heart could tell.

SELECTIONS FROM THE PRELUDE

I. The Discipline of Nature

Dust as we are, the immortal spirit grows
Like harmony in music; there is a dark
Inscrutable workmanship that reconciles
Discordant elements, makes them cling together
In one society. How strange that all 5
The terrors, pains, and early miseries,
Regrets, vexations, lassitudes interfused
Within my mind, should e'er have borne a part,
And that a needful part, in making up
The calm existence that is mine when I 10
Am worthy of myself! Praise to the end!
Thanks to the means which Nature deigned to employ;

Whether her fearless visitings, or those
That came with soft alarm, like hurtless light
Opening the peaceful clouds; or she would use 15
Severer interventions, ministry
More palpable, as best might suit her aim.
   One summer evening (led by her) I found
A little boat tied to a willow tree
Within a rocky cave, its usual home. 20
Straight I unloosed her chain, and stepping in
Pushed from the shore. It was an act of stealth
And troubled pleasure, nor without the voice
Of mountain-echoes did my boat move on;
Leaving behind her still, on either side, 25
Small circles glittering idly in the moon,
Until they melted all into one track
Of sparkling light. But now, like one who rows,
Proud of his skill, to reach a chosen point
With an unswerving line, I fixed my view 30
Upon the summit of a craggy ridge,
The horizon's utmost boundary; far above
Was nothing but the stars and the grey sky.
She was an elfin pinnace; lustily
I dipped my oars into the silent lake, 35
And, as I rose upon the stroke, my boat
Went heaving through the water like a swan;
When, from behind that craggy steep till then
The horizon's bound, a huge peak, black and huge,
As if with voluntary power instinct, 40
Upreared its head. I struck and struck again,

And growing still in stature the grim shape
Towered up between me and the stars, and still,
For so it seemed, with purpose of its own
And measured motion like a living thing, 45
Strode after me. With trembling oars I turned,
And through the silent water stole my way
Back to the covert of the willow tree;
There in her mooring-place I left my bark,—
And through the meadows homeward went, in grave 50
And serious mood; but after I had seen
That spectacle, for many days, my brain
Worked with a dim and undetermined sense
Of unknown modes of being; o'er my thoughts
There hung a darkness, call it solitude 55
Or blank desertion. No familiar shapes
Remained, no pleasant images of trees,
Of sea or sky, no colours of green fields;
But huge and mighty forms, that do not live
Like living men, moved slowly through the mind 60
By day, and were a trouble to my dreams.
Wisdom and Spirit of the universe!
Thou Soul that art the eternity of thought,
That givest to forms and images a breath
And everlasting motion, not in vain 65
By day or star-light thus from my first dawn
Of childhood didst thou intertwine for me
The passions that build up our human soul;
Not with the mean and vulgar works of man,
But with high objects, with enduring things— 70

With life and nature—purifying thus
The elements of feeling and of thought,
And sanctifying, by such discipline,
Both pain and fear, until we recognise
A grandeur in the beatings of the heart. 75
Nor was this fellowship vouchsafed to me
With stinted kindness. In November days,
When vapours rolling down the valley made
A lonely scene more lonesome, among woods,
At noon and 'mid the calm of summer nights, 80
When, by the margin of the trembling lake,
Beneath the gloomy hills homeward I went
In solitude, such intercourse was mine;
Mine was it in the fields both day and night,
And by the waters, all the summer long. 85
And in the frosty season, when the sun
Was set, and visible for many a mile
The cottage windows blazed through twilight gloom,
I heeded not their summons: happy time
It was indeed for all of us—for me 90
It was a time of rapture! Clear and loud
The village clock tolled six,—I wheeled about,
Proud and exulting like an untired horse
That cares not for his home. All shod with steel,
We hissed along the polished ice in games 95
Confederate, imitative of the chase
And woodland pleasures,—the resounding horn,
The pack loud chiming, and the hunted hare.
So through the darkness and the cold we flew,

And not a voice was idle; with the din 100
Smitten, the precipices rang aloud;
The leafless trees and every icy crag
Tinkled like iron; while far distant hills
Into the tumult sent an alien sound
Of melancholy not unnoticed, while the stars 105
Eastward were sparkling clear, and in the west
The orange sky of evening died away.
Not seldom from the uproar I retired
Into a silent bay, or sportively
Glanced sideway, leaving the tumultuous throng, 110
To cut across the reflex of a star
That fled, and flying still before me, gleamed
Upon the glassy plain; and oftentimes,
When we had given our bodies to the wind,
And all the shadowy banks on either side 115
Came sweeping through the darkness, spinning still
The rapid line of motion, then at once
Have I, reclining back upon my heels,
Stopped short; yet still the solitary cliffs
Wheeled by me—even as if the earth had rolled 120
With visible motion her diurnal round!
Behind me did they stretch in solemn train,
Feebler and feebler, and I stood and watched
Till all was tranquil as a dreamless sleep.
Ye Presences of Nature in the sky 125
And on the earth! Ye Visions of the hills!
And Souls of lonely places! can I think
A vulgar hope was yours when ye employed

Such ministry, when ye, through many a year
Haunting me thus among my boyish sports, 130
On eaves and trees, upon the woods and hills,
Impressed upon all forms the characters
Of danger or desire; and thus did make
The surface of the universal earth
With triumph and delight, with hope and fear, 135
Work like a sea?

II. Nature the Source of Hope and Courage

If this be error, and another faith
Find easier access to the pious mind,
Yet were I grossly destitute of all
Those human sentiments that make this earth
So dear, if I should fail with grateful voice 5
To speak of you, ye mountains, and ye lakes
And sounding cataracts, ye mists and winds
That dwell among the hills where I was born.
If in my youth I have been pure in heart,
If, mingling with the world, I am content 10
With my own modest pleasures, and have lived
With God and Nature communing, removed
From little enmities and low desires,
The gift is yours; if in these times of fear,
This melancholy waste of hopes o'erthrown, 15
If, 'mid indifference and apathy,
And wicked exultation when good men
On every side fall off, we know not how,

To selfishness, disguised in gentle names
Of peace and quiet and domestic love, 20
Yet mingled not unwillingly with sneers
On visionary minds; if, in this time
Of dereliction and dismay, I yet
Despair not of our nature, but retain
A more than Roman confidence, a faith 25
That fails not, in all sorrow my support,
The blessing of my life; the gift is yours,
Ye winds and sounding cataracts! 'tis yours,
Ye mountains! thine, O Nature! Thou hast fed
My lofty speculations; and in thee, 30
For this uneasy heart of ours, I find
A never-failing principle of joy
And purest passion.

III. St John's College, Cambridge

The Evangelist St John my patron was:
Three Gothic courts are his, and in the first
Was my abiding-place, a nook obscure;
Right underneath, the College kitchens made
A humming sound, less tuneable than bees, 5
But hardly less industrious; with shrill notes
Of sharp command and scolding intermixed.
Near me hung Trinity's loquacious clock,
Who never let the quarters, night or day,
Slip by him unproclaimed, and told the hours 10
Twice over with a male and female voice.

Her pealing organ was my neighbour too;
And from my pillow, looking forth by light
Of moon or favouring stars, I could behold
The antechapel where the statue stood 15
Of Newton with his prism and silent face,
The marble index of a mind for ever
Voyaging through strange seas of thought, alone.

IV. A Summer Dawn

Ere we retired,
The cock had crowed, and now the eastern sky
Was kindling, not unseen, from humble copse
And open field, through which the pathway wound,
And homeward led my steps. Magnificent 5
The morning rose, in memorable pomp,
Glorious as e'er I had beheld—in front,
The sea lay laughing at a distance; near,
The solid mountains shone, bright as the clouds,
Grain-tinctured, drenched in empyrean light; 10
And in the meadows and the lower grounds
Was all the sweetness of a common dawn—
Dews, vapours, and the melody of birds,
And labourers going forth to till the fields.
Ah! need I say, dear Friend! that to the brim 15
My heart was full; I made no vows, but vows
Were then made for me; bond unknown to me
Was given, that I should be, else sinning greatly,
A dedicated Spirit. On I walked
In thankful blessedness, which yet survives. 20

V. The Boy of Windermere

There was a Boy: ye knew him well, ye cliffs
And islands of Winander!—many a time
At evening, when the earliest stars began
To move along the edges of the hills,
Rising or setting, would he stand alone 5
Beneath the trees or by the glimmering lake,
And there, with fingers interwoven, both hands
Pressed closely palm to palm, and to his mouth
Uplifted, he, as through an instrument,
Blew mimic hootings to the silent owls, 10
That they might answer him; and they would shout
Across the watery vale, and shout again,
Responsive to his call, with quivering peals,
And long halloos and screams, and echoes loud,
Redoubled and redoubled, concourse wild 15
Of jocund din; and, when a lengthened pause
Of silence came and baffled his best skill,
Then sometimes, in that silence while he hung
Listening, a gentle shock of mild surprise
Has carried far into his heart the voice 20
Of mountain torrents; or the visible scene
Would enter unawares into his mind,
With all its solemn imagery, its rocks,
Its woods, and that uncertain heaven, received
Into the bosom of the steady lake. 25
This Boy was taken from his mates, and died
In childhood, ere he was full twelve years old.

Fair is the spot, most beautiful the vale
Where he was born; the grassy churchyard hangs
Upon a slope above the village school, 30
And through that churchyard when my way has led
On summer evenings, I believe that there
A long half hour together I have stood
Mute, looking at the grave in which he lies!

VI. The Simplon Pass

The brook and road
Were fellow-travellers in this gloomy strait,
And with them did we journey several hours
At a slow pace. The immeasurable height
Of woods decaying, never to be decayed, 5
The stationary blasts of waterfalls,
And in the narrow rent at every turn
Winds thwarting winds, bewildered and forlorn,
The torrents shooting from the clear blue sky,
The rocks that muttered close upon our ears, 10
Black drizzling crags that spake by the way-side
As if a voice were in them, the sick sight
And giddy prospect of the raving stream,
The unfettered clouds and region of the Heavens,
Tumult and peace, the darkness and the light— 15
Were all like workings of one mind, the features
Of the same face, blossoms upon one tree;
Characters of the great Apocalypse,
The types and symbols of Eternity,
Of first, and last, and midst, and without end. 20

VII. Ascent of Snowdon

It was a close, warm, breezeless summer night,
Wan, dull, and glaring with a dripping fog
Low-hung and thick that covered all the sky;
But, undiscouraged, we began to climb
The mountain-side. The mist soon girt us round, 5
And, after ordinary travellers' talk
With our conductor, pensively we sank
Each into commerce with his private thoughts:
Thus did we breast the ascent, and by myself
Was nothing either seen or heard that checked 10
Those musings or diverted, save that once
The shepherd's lurcher, who, among the crags,
Had to his joy unearthed a hedgehog, teased
His coiled-up prey with barkings turbulent.
This small adventure, for even such it seemed 15
In that wild place and at the dead of night,
Being over and forgotten, on we wound
In silence as before. With forehead bent
Earthward, as if in opposition set
Against an enemy, I panted up 20
With eager pace, and no less eager thoughts.
Thus might we wear a midnight hour away,
Ascending at loose distance each from each,
And I, as chanced, the foremost of the band;
When at my feet the ground appeared to brighten, 25
And with a step or two seemed brighter still;
Nor was time given to ask or learn the cause,

For instantly a light upon the turf
Fell like a flash, and lo! as I looked up,
The Moon hung naked in a firmament 30
Of azure without cloud, and at my feet
Rested a silent sea of hoary mist.
A hundred hills their dusky backs upheaved
All over this still ocean; and beyond,
Far, far beyond, the solid vapours stretched, 35
In headlands, tongues, and promontory shapes,
Into the main Atlantic, that appeared
To dwindle, and give up his majesty,
Usurped upon so far as the sight could reach.
Not so the ethereal vault; encroachment none 40
Was there, nor loss; only the inferior stars
Had disappeared, or shed a fainter light
In the clear presence of the full-orbed Moon,
Who, from her sovereign elevation, gazed
Upon the billowy ocean, as it lay 45
All meek and silent, save that through a rift—
Not distant from the shore whereon we stood,
A fixed, abysmal, gloomy, breathing-place—
Mounted the roar of waters, torrents, streams
Innumerable, roaring with one voice! 50
Heard over earth and sea, and, in that hour,
For so it seemed, felt by the starry heavens.

VIII. Dorothy Wordsworth and Coleridge

Child of my parents! Sister of my soul!
Thanks in sincerest verse have been elsewhere
Poured out for all the early tenderness
Which I from thee imbibed: and 'tis most true
That later seasons owed to thee no less; 5
For, spite of thy sweet influence and the touch
Of kindred hands that opened out the springs
Of genial thought in childhood, and in spite
Of all that unassisted I had marked
In life or Nature of those charms minute 10
That win their way into the heart by stealth,
Still (to the very going-out of youth)
I too exclusively esteemed *that* love,
And sought *that* beauty, which, as Milton sings,
Hath terror in it. Thou didst soften down 15
This over-sternness; but for thee, dear Friend!
My soul, too reckless of mild grace, had stood
In her original self too confident,
Retained too long a countenance severe;
A rock with torrents roaring, with the clouds 20
Familiar, and a favourite of the stars:
But thou didst plant its crevices with flowers,
Hang it with shrubs that twinkle in the breeze,
And teach the little birds to build their nests
And warble in its chambers. At a time 25
When Nature, destined to remain so long
Foremost in my affections, had fallen back

Into a second place, pleased to become
A handmaid to a nobler than herself,
When every day brought with it some new sense 30
Of exquisite regard for common things,
And all the earth was budding with these gifts
Of more refined humanity, thy breath,
Dear Sister! was a kind of gentler spring
That went before my steps. Thereafter came 35
One whom with thee friendship had early paired;
She came, no more a phantom to adorn
A moment, but an inmate of the heart,
And yet a spirit, there for me enshrined
To penetrate the lofty and the low; 40
Even as one essence of pervading light
Shines, in the brightest of ten thousand stars,
And, the meek worm that feeds her lonely lamp
Couched in the dewy grass.

With such a theme,
Coleridge! with this my argument, of thee 45
Shall I be silent? O capacious Soul!
Placed on this earth to love and understand,
And from thy presence shed the light of love,
Shall I be mute, ere thou be spoken of?
Thy kindred influence to my heart of hearts 50
Did also find its way. Thus fear relaxed
Her overweening grasp; thus thoughts and things
In the self-haunting spirit learned to take
More rational proportions; mystery,
The incumbent mystery of sense and soul, 55

Of life and death, time and eternity,
Admitted more habitually a mild
Interposition—a serene delight
In closelier gathering cares, such as become
A human creature, howsoe'er endowed, 60
Poet, or destined for a humbler name;
And so the deep enthusiastic joy,
The rapture of the hallelujah sent
From all that breathes and is, was chastened, stemmed
And balanced by pathetic truth, by trust 65
In hopeful reason, leaning on the stay
Of Providence; and in reverence for duty,
Here, if need be, struggling with storms, and there
Strewing in peace life's humblest ground with herbs,
At every season green, sweet at all hours. 70

SELECTIONS FROM THE EXCURSION

I. The Wanderer's Boyhood

From his sixth year, the Boy of whom I speak,
In summer, tended cattle on the hills;
But, through the inclement and the perilous days
Of long-continuing winter, he repaired,
Equipped with satchel, to a school, that stood 5
Sole building on a mountain's dreary edge,
Remote from view of city spire, or sound
Of minster clock! From that bleak tenement
He, many an evening, to his distant home
In solitude returning, saw the hills 10

Grow larger in the darkness; all alone
Beheld the stars come out above his head,
And travelled through the wood, with no one near
To whom he might confess the things he saw.
So the foundations of his mind were laid. 15
In such communion, not from terror free,
While yet a child, and long before his time,
Had he perceived the presence and the power
Of greatness; and deep feelings had impressed
So vividly great objects that they lay 20
Upon his mind like substances, whose presence
Perplexed the bodily sense. He had received
A precious gift; for, as he grew in years,
With these impressions would he still compare
All his remembrances, thoughts, shapes, and forms; 25
And, being still unsatisfied with aught
Of dimmer character, he thence attained
An active power to fasten images
Upon his brain; and on their pictured lines
Intensely brooded, even till they acquired 30
The liveliness of dreams. Nor did he fail,
While yet a child, with a child's eagerness
Incessantly to turn his ear and eye
On all things which the moving seasons brought
To feed such appetite—nor this alone 35
Appeased his yearning:—in the after-day
Of boyhood, many an hour in caves forlorn,
And 'mid the hollow depths of naked crags
He sate, and even in their fixed lineaments,

Or from the power of a peculiar eye, 40
Or by creative feeling overborne,
Or by predominance of thought oppressed,
Even in their fixed and steady lineaments
He traced an ebbing and a flowing mind,
Expression ever varying!
Thus informed, 45
He had small need of books; for many a tale
Traditionary round the mountains hung,
And many a legend, peopling the dark woods,
Nourished Imagination in her growth,
And gave the Mind that apprehensive power 50
By which she is made quick to recognise
The moral properties and scope of things.
But eagerly he read, and read again,
Whate'er the minister's old shelf supplied;
The life and death of martyrs, who sustained, 55
With will inflexible, those fearful pangs
Triumphantly displayed in records left
Of persecution, and the Covenant-times
Whose echo rings through Scotland to this hour!
And there, by lucky hap, had been preserved 60
A straggling volume, torn and incomplete,
That left half-told the preternatural tale,
Romance of giants, chronicle of fiends,
Profuse in garniture of wooden cuts
Strange and uncouth; dire faces, figures dire, 65
Sharp-kneed, sharp-elbowed, and lean-ankled too,
With long and ghostly shanks—forms which once seen

Could never be forgotten!

In his heart,
Where Fear sate thus, a cherished visitant,
Was wanting yet the pure delight of love 70
By sound diffused, or by the breathing air,
Or by the silent looks of happy things,
Or flowing from the universal face
Of earth and sky. But he had felt the power
Of Nature, and already was prepared, 75
By his intense conceptions, to receive
Deeply the lesson deep of love which he,
Whom Nature, by whatever means, has taught
To feel intensely, cannot but receive.

II. The Valley of Blea Tarn

Diverging now (as if his quest had been
Some secret of the mountains, cavern, fall
Of water, or some lofty eminence,
Renowned for splendid prospect far and wide)
We scaled, without a track to ease our steps, 5
A steep ascent; and reached a dreary plain,
With a tumultuous waste of huge hill tops
Before us; savage region! which I paced
Dispirited: when, all at once, behold!
Beneath our feet, a little lowly vale, 10
A lowly vale, and yet uplifted high
Among the mountains; even as if the spot
Had been from eldest time by wish of theirs

So placed, to be shut out from all the world!
Urn-like it was in shape, deep as an urn; 15
With rocks encompassed, save that to the south
Was one small opening, where a heath-clad ridge
Supplied a boundary less abrupt and close;
A quiet treeless nook, with two green fields,
A liquid pool that glittered in the sun, 20
And one bare dwelling; one abode, no more!
It seemed the home of poverty and toil,
Though not of want: the little fields, made green
By husbandry of many thrifty years,
Paid cheerful tribute to the moorland house. 25
—There crows the cock, single in his domain:
The small birds find in spring no thicket there
To shroud them; only from the neighbouring vales
The cuckoo, straggling up to the hill tops,
Shouteth faint tidings of some gladder place. 30

III. The Langdale Pikes

In genial mood,
While at our pastoral banquet thus we sate
Fronting the window of that little cell,
I could not, ever and anon, forbear
To glance an upward look on two huge Peaks, 5
That from some other vale peered into this.
'Those lusty twins,' exclaimed our host, 'If here
It were your lot to dwell, would soon become
Your prized companions.—Many are the notes

Which, in his tuneful course, the wind draws forth 10
From rocks, woods, caverns, heaths, and dashing shores;
And well those lofty brethren bear their part
In the wild concert—chiefly when the storm
Rides high; then all the upper air they fill
With roaring sound, that ceases not to flow, 15
Like smoke, along the level of the blast,
In mighty current; theirs, too, is the song
Of stream and headlong flood that seldom fails;
And, in the grim and breathless hour of noon,
Methinks that I have heard them echo back 20
The thunder's greeting. Nor have Nature's laws
Left them ungifted with a power to yield
Music of finer tone; a harmony,
So do I call it, though it be the hand
Of silence, though there be no voice;—the clouds, 25
The mist, the shadows, light of golden suns,
Motions of moonlight, all come thither—touch,
And have an answer—thither come, and shape
A language not unwelcome to sick hearts
And idle spirits:—there the sun himself, 30
At the calm close of summer's longest day,
Rests his substantial orb;—between those heights
And on the top of either pinnacle,
More keenly than elsewhere in night's blue vault,
Sparkle the stars, as of their station proud. 35
Thoughts are not busier in the mind of man
Than the mute agents stirring there:—alone
Here do I sit and watch.—'

IV. The French Revolution

From that abstraction I was roused,—and how?
Even as a thoughtful shepherd by a flash
Of lightning startled in a gloomy cave
Of these wild hills. For, lo! the dread Bastille,
With all the chambers in its horrid towers, 5
Fell to the ground:—by violence overthrown
Of indignation; and with shouts that drowned
The crash it made in falling! From the wreck
A golden palace rose, or seemed to rise,
The appointed seat of equitable law 10
And mild paternal sway. The potent shock
I felt: the transformation I perceived,
As marvellously seized as in that moment
When, from the blind mist issuing, I beheld
Glory—beyond all glory ever seen, 15
Confusion infinite of heaven and earth,
Dazzling the soul. Meanwhile, prophetic harps
In every grove were ringing, 'War shall cease;
Did ye not hear that conquest is abjured?
Bring garlands, bring forth choicest flowers, to deck 20
The tree of Liberty.'—My heart rebounded;
My melancholy voice the chorus joined;
—'Be joyful all ye nations; in all lands,
Ye that are capable of joy be glad!
Henceforth, whate'er is wanting to yourselves 25
In others ye shall promptly find;—and all,

Enriched by mutual and reflected wealth,
Shall with one heart honour their common kind.'
  Thus was I reconverted to the world;
Society became my glittering bride, 30
And airy hopes my children.—From the depths
Of natural passion, seemingly escaped,
My soul diffused herself in wide embrace
Of institutions, and the forms of things;
As they exist, in mutable array, 35
Upon life's surface. What, though in my veins
There flowed no Gallic blood, nor had I breathed
The air of France, not less than Gallic zeal
Kindled and burnt among the sapless twigs
Of my exhausted heart. If busy men 40
In sober conclave met, to weave a web
Of amity, whose living threads should stretch
Beyond the seas, and to the farthest pole,
There did I sit, assisting. If, with noise
And acclamation, crowds in open air 45
Expressed the tumult of their minds, my voice
There mingled, heard or not. The powers of song
I left not uninvoked; and, in still groves,
Where mild enthusiasts tuned a pensive lay
Of thanks and expectation, in accord 50
With their belief, I sang Saturnian rule
Returned,—a progeny of golden years
Permitted to descend, and bless mankind.

V. Natural Religion in Greece

In that fair clime, the lonely herdsman, stretched
On the soft grass through half a summer's day,
With music lulled his indolent repose:
And, in some fit of weariness, if he,
When his own breath was silent, chanced to hear 5
A distant strain, far sweeter than the sounds
Which his poor skill could make, his fancy fetched,
Even from the blazing chariot of the sun,
A beardless Youth, who touched a golden lute,
And filled the illumined groves with ravishment. 10
The nightly hunter, lifting a bright eye
Up towards the crescent moon, with grateful heart
Called on the lovely wanderer who bestowed
That timely light, to share his joyous sport:
And hence, a beaming Goddess with her Nymphs, 15
Across the lawn and through the darksome grove,
Not unaccompanied by tuneful notes
By echo multiplied from rock or cave,
Swept in the storm of chase; as moon and stars
Glance rapidly along the clouded heaven, 20
When winds are blowing strong. The traveller slaked
His thirst from rill or gushing fount, and thanked
The Naiad. Sunbeams, upon distant hills
Gliding apace, with shadows in their train,
Might, with small help from fancy, be transformed 25
Into fleet Oreads sporting visibly.
The Zephyrs fanning, as they passed, their wings,

Lacked not, for love, fair objects whom they wooed
With gentle whisper. Withered boughs grotesque,
Stripped of their leaves and twigs by hoary age, 30
From depth of shaggy covert peeping forth
In the low vale, or on steep mountain-side;
And, sometimes, intermixed with stirring horns
Of the live deer, or goat's depending beard,—
These were the lurking Satyrs, a wild brood 35
Of gamesome Deities; or Pan himself,
The simple shepherd's awe-inspiring God!

VI. The Inward Power of the Soul

Within the soul a faculty abides,
That with interpositions, which would hide
And darken, so can deal that they become
Contingencies of pomp; and serve to exalt
Her native brightness. As the ample moon, 5
In the deep stillness of a summer even
Rising behind a thick and lofty grove,
Burns, like an unconsuming fire of light,
In the green trees; and, kindling on all sides
Their leafy umbrage, turns the dusky veil 10
Into a substance glorious as her own,
Yea, with her own incorporated, by power
Capacious and serene. Like power abides
In man's celestial spirit; virtue thus
Sets forth and magnifies herself; thus feeds 15
A calm, a beautiful, and silent fire,

From the encumbrances of mortal life,
From error, disappointment—nay, from guilt;
And sometimes, so relenting justice wills,
From palpable oppressions of despair. 20

VII. The Voices of Nature

Has not the soul, the being of your life,
Received a shock of awful consciousness,
In some calm season, when these lofty rocks
At night's approach bring down the unclouded sky,
To rest upon their circumambient walls; 5
A temple framing of dimensions vast,
And yet not too enormous for the sound
Of human anthems,—choral song, or burst
Sublime of instrumental harmony,
To glorify the Eternal! What if these 10
Did never break the stillness that prevails
Here,—if the solemn nightingale be mute,
And the soft woodlark here did never chant
Her vespers,—Nature fails not to provide
Impulse and utterance. The whispering air 15
Sends inspiration from the shadowy heights,
And blind recesses of the caverned rocks:
The little rills, and waters numberless,
Inaudible by daylight, blend their notes
With the loud streams: and often, at the hour 20
When issue forth the first pale stars, is heard,
Within the circuit of this fabric huge,

One voice—the solitary raven, flying
Athwart the concave of the dark blue dome,
Unseen, perchance above all power of sight— 25
An iron knell! with echoes from afar
Faint—and still fainter—as the cry, with which
The wanderer accompanies her flight
Through the calm region, fades upon the ear,
Diminishing by distance till it seemed 30
To expire; yet from the abyss is caught again,
And yet again recovered!

VIII. The Deaf Dalesman

Almost at the root
Of that tall pine, the shadow of whose bare
And slender stem, while here I sit at eve,
Oft stretches toward me, like a long straight path
Traced faintly in the greensward; there, beneath 5
A plain blue stone, a gentle Dalesman lies,
From whom, in early childhood, was withdrawn
The precious gift of hearing. He grew up
From year to year in loneliness of soul;
And this deep mountain-valley was to him 10
Soundless, with all its streams. The bird of dawn
Did never rouse this Cottager from sleep
With startling summons; not for his delight
The vernal cuckoo shouted; not for him
Murmured the labouring bee. When stormy winds 15
Were working the broad bosom of the lake

Into a thousand thousand sparkling waves,
Rocking the trees, or driving cloud on cloud
Along the sharp edge of yon lofty crags,
The agitated scene before his eye 20
Was silent as a picture: evermore
Were all things silent, wheresoe'er he moved.
Yet, by the solace of his own pure thoughts
Upheld, he duteously pursued the round
Of rural labours; the steep mountain-side 25
Ascended, with his staff and faithful dog;
The plough he guided, and the scythe he swayed;
And the ripe corn before his sickle fell
Among the jocund reapers. For himself,
All watchful and industrious as he was, 30
He wrought not: neither field nor flock he owned:
No wish for wealth had place within his mind;
Nor husband's love, nor father's hope or care.
Though born a younger brother, need was none
That from the floor of his paternal home 35
He should depart, to plant himself anew.
And when, mature in manhood, he beheld
His parents laid in earth, no loss ensued
Of rights to him; but he remained well pleased,
By the pure bond of independent love, 40
An inmate of a second family;
The fellow-labourer and friend of him
To whom the small inheritance had fallen.
—Nor deem that his mild presence was a weight
That pressed upon his brother's house; for books 45

Were ready comrades whom he could not tire;
Of whose society the blameless Man
Was never satiate. Their familiar voice,
Even to old age, with unabated charm
Beguiled his leisure hours; refreshed his thoughts; 50
Beyond its natural elevation raised
His introverted spirit; and bestowed
Upon his life an outward dignity
Which all acknowledged. The dark winter night,
The stormy day, each had its own resource; 55
Song of the muses, sage historic tale,
Science severe, or word of holy Writ
Announcing immortality and joy
To the assembled spirits of just men
Made perfect, and from injury secure. 60
—Thus soothed at home, thus busy in the field,
To no perverse suspicion he gave way,
No languor, peevishness, or vain complaint:
And they, who were about him, did not fail
In reverence, or in courtesy; they prized 65
His gentle manners: and his peaceful smiles,
The gleams of his slow-varying countenance,
Were met with answering sympathy and love.
—At length, when sixty years and five were told,
A slow disease insensibly consumed 70
The powers of nature: and a few short steps
Of friends and kindred bore him from his home
(Yon cottage shaded by the woody crags)
To the profounder stillness of the grave.

—Nor was his funeral denied the grace 75
Of many tears, virtuous and thoughtful grief;
Heart-sorrow rendered sweet by gratitude.
And now that monumental stone preserves
His name, and unambitiously relates
How long, and by what kindly outward aids, 80
And in what pure contentedness of mind,
The sad privation was by him endured.
—And yon tall pine-tree, whose composing sound
Was wasted on the good Man's living ear,
Hath now its own peculiar sanctity; 85
And, at the touch of every wandering breeze,
Murmurs, not idly, o'er his peaceful grave.

IX. Sunset and Summer Haze

Already had the sun,
Sinking with less than ordinary state,
Attained his western bound; but rays of light—
Now suddenly diverging from the orb
Retired behind the mountain-tops or veiled 5
By the dense air—shot upwards to the crown
Of the blue firmament—aloft, and wide:
And multitudes of little floating clouds,
Through their ethereal texture pierced—ere we,
Who saw, of change were conscious—had become 10
Vivid as fire; clouds separately poised,—
Innumerable multitude of forms

Scattered through half the circle of the sky;
And giving back, and shedding each on each,
With prodigal communion, the bright hues 15
Which from the unapparent fount of glory
They had imbibed, and ceased not to receive.
That which the heavens displayed, the liquid deep
Repeated; but with unity sublime!

NOTES

REMEMBRANCE OF COLLINS

These three stanzas originally formed one poem with two others which are now entitled *Lines written while sailing in a boat at evening*. They were composed in 1789 and first published in 1798. Although the poem was actually composed beside the Cam at Cambridge, William Collins' (1721-59) *Ode on the Death of Mr Thomson*, the scene of which ' is supposed to lie on the Thames, near Richmond,' suggested its theme and title.

5–8. Wordsworth was obviously thinking of sir John Denham's famous lines, *Cooper's Hill*, 189-92:

> O could I flow like thee, and make thy stream
> My great example, as it is my theme!
> Though deep, yet clear; though gentle, yet not dull;
> Strong without rage, without o'erflowing full.

13–16. The end of Collins' life was darkened by insanity. His beautiful ode on Thomson, a cardinal example of that ' skill to complain ' and to awaken feelings of pity in others which he possessed, was apparently written upon the Thames, within sight of the spire of Richmond church, where Thomson, the author of *The Seasons*, was buried. Thomson is peculiarly associated with Richmond, where the later years of his life were spent: he died there in 1748.

14. **later**] Wordsworth notes that Collins' ode on Thomson was ' the last written, I believe, of the poems which were published during his life-time.' The comparative degree therefore distinguishes the maturity of Collins' poem from the conscious youthfulness of Wordsworth's attempt to follow him.

18. *See Ode on the Death of Mr Thomson*, 13–16:
Remembrance oft shall haunt the shore
When Thames in summer wreaths is drest;
And oft suspend the dashing oar
To bid his gentle spirit rest!

23. **The evening darkness**] Cf. *ibid.* 33, 34:
And see, the fairy valleys fade,
Dun Night has veil'd the solemn view.

EXPOSTULATION AND REPLY

This poem and the companion piece, *The Tables Turned*, were composed at Alfoxden in the spring of 1798 and were published in *Lyrical Ballads*, later in the same year. Wordsworth contrasts the learning derived from books with that to be derived from Nature by the willing mind. In the classified editions of his poems, these two form Nos. I and II of Poems of Sentiment and Reflection.

13. **Esthwaite lake**] The lake at the head of which Hawkshead, the scene of Wordsworth's school-days, is situated.

15. **Matthew**] A person introduced several times into his early poems by Wordsworth, and explained by him elsewhere as compounded from various characters of his acquaintance.

21. **Powers**] The invisible forces of Nature. Cf. *To the Rev. Dr Wordsworth*, 29, p. 68 above; ' these rustic Powers.'

THE TABLES TURNED

See introd. note to the preceding poem.

21. Cf. the stanzas *To my Sister* (' It is the first mild day of March '), written about the same time, ll. 25-8:

One moment now may give us more
Than years of toiling reason:
Our minds shall drink at every pore
The spirit of the season.

LINES

COMPOSED A FEW MILES ABOVE TINTERN ABBEY

Published in *Lyrical Ballads*, 1798, some two months after its composition. Wordsworth writes, 'I began it upon leaving Tintern, after crossing the Wye, and concluded it just as I was entering Bristol in the evening, after a ramble of four or five days, with my Sister. Not a line of it was altered, and not any part of it written down till I reached Bristol.' The visit to Tintern called forth reminiscences of an earlier visit in the summer of 1793 and led Wordsworth to review the change which had affected his attitude to Nature during the interval. The intellectual progress described in these lines was afterwards traced more fully in *The Prelude*. Apart from its personal interest, *Tintern Abbey* possesses a special historical value as the first clear statement of the emotional change in poetry of which the Romantic movement was the climax, recognising and defining the power of Nature to quicken and sustain the imagination and creative faculty. Classified among Poems of the Imagination (No. xxvi).

1–22. The scene, in the narrow gorge of the Wye somewhere between Tintern and Monmouth, is described with emphasis upon the mingling of seclusion with the sense of the presence of man.

17. **wreaths of smoke**] Cf. the sonnet *Not Love, not War* written in 1823, ll. 5–8:

> But where untroubled peace and concord dwell,
> There also is the Muse not loth to range,
> Watching the twilight smoke of cot or grange,
> Skyward ascending from a woody dell.

21. **some Hermit's cave**] In eighteenth-century poetry the hermit was constantly introduced to give effect to pictures of solitude. See, e.g., Parnell's *The Hermit*, and the use of hermits as poetical ornaments in such poems as Jago's *Edge-Hill*. Wordsworth retains this convention and uses it frequently: Coleridge

used it in *The Ancient Mariner* and Scott was fully alive to its picturesque value in *The Lady of the Lake*, *Ivanhoe*, etc.

22–57. Reviewing the interval of time since his last visit and appealing to his own experience, Wordsworth expresses the power of the remembrance of beautiful scenes to console amid weariness, to affect and humanise life and to lift man above his bodily needs and the perplexities of the concrete world, by withdrawing his mind into the region of abstract thought.

34, 35. See *Excursion*, I, 191–6 (selection I, 74-9, p. 94 above), where Wordsworth traces the gradual growth of the influence of Nature upon his Wanderer, after commenting upon his imperfect apprehension of her power in early life.

47. **an eye made quiet**] Cf. *A Poet's Epitaph* (1799), 45–52:

> The outward shows of sky and earth,
> Of hill and valley, he has viewed;
> And impulses of deeper birth
> Have come to him in solitude.
>
> In common things that round us lie
> Some random truths he can impart,—
> The harvest of a quiet eye
> That broods and sleeps on his own heart.

58–111. Five years have worked a change in his spirit. Then his mind, awakening to the power of Nature, was conscious of the fear she inspires rather than of the love she instils. The pleasures of the eye and ear absorbed him, to the exclusion of those of the heart. The freshness of the rapture with which he welcomed half-understood sights and sounds has left him for ever, but in compensation he has learned, by spiritual communion with Nature, to feel a closer kinship with humanity and to realise the power of an indwelling vital principle which includes the whole of Nature and human life in its workings.

71. **something that he dreads**] The awakening of the vivid consciousness of fear in the presence of natural forces which oppress the mind (*Excursion*, I, 138, 139) 'like substances,

whose presence perplexed the bodily sense' is described in *The Prelude*, I, 357-400. Cf. also *Excursion*, I, 185 sqq. (selection I, 68 sqq., p. 94 above). In *Prelude*, XIV, 162, Wordsworth ascribes his attainment of moral balance to the workings of fear and love produced by his intercourse with Nature:

to fear and love,
To love as prime and chief, for there fear ends.

91. *Prelude*, VIII, takes as its secondary title 'Love of Nature leading to love of Man.' This principle is illustrated abundantly in such poems as *Michael* and *Ruth*. Cf. *The Tables Turned*, 21–4 (p. 4 above).

94–102. Cf. this noble acknowledgement of the presence of a divine spirit in all Nature with the lines 'Wisdom and Spirit of the Universe' (*Prelude*, I, 401 sqq.), p. 79 above. This presence is the source of life in Nature and of the power of Nature to console and encourage. Wordsworth's doctrine is identical with that contained in the Wisdom of Solomon: see, e.g., Wisdom vii, 24, 25, and viii, 1; and cf. i, 7. Cf. also the doctrine of Greek philosophy, expounded by Anaxagoras, that νοῦς, the immortal principle of mind, acting upon the particles of matter, was the arranger and cause of all things (ὁ διακοσμῶν τε καὶ πάντων αἴτιος: Plato, *Phaedo*, 97 c). Wordsworth repeats the sentiment of these lines in the opening of *Excursion*, book IX, where the Wanderer asserts the presence of an active principle in every form of being:

Spirit that knows no insulated spot,
No chasm, no solitude; from link to link
It circulates, the Soul of all the worlds.

'Its most apparent home,' he proceeds to say, 'is the human mind where it nevertheless is reverenced least, and least respected.'

106. Wordsworth notes: 'This line has a close resemblance to an admirable line of Young's, the exact expression of which I do not recollect.' He seems to allude to *Night Thoughts*, VI, 427, where Young says of the senses that they 'half create the wondrous world we see.'

110–59. For the final address to his sister, encouraging her in her communion with Nature, cf. *Prelude*, XIV, 232-66, where her influence upon him is gratefully recorded. Dorothy Wordsworth's sensibility to natural beauty is manifested in her *Journals*, large portions of which have been edited by professor Knight. Her power of detailed description and ability to catch the spirit of the scenery under observation have few parallels in English prose.

119. **thy wild eyes**] De Quincey, *Reminiscences of the Lake Poets*, gives a vivid description of Dorothy Wordsworth. 'Her eyes were not soft, as Mrs Wordsworth's, nor were they fierce or bold; but they were wild and startling, and hurried in their motion.'

122, 123. Cf. *Excursion*, IX, 111–13:

> one maternal spirit, bringing forth
> And cherishing with ever-constant love,
> That tires not, nor betrays.

125. **she can so inform**] Cf. the exquisite expression of the power of Nature to mould mind and feature to her influences in 'Three years she grew in sun and shower' (p. 11 above).

134. **Therefore let the moon**] Cf. *Coleridge's description* in *The Nightingale* of Dorothy's solitary walks by moonlight in the woods at Nether Stowey:

> Even like a Lady vowed and dedicate
> To something more than Nature in the grove.

FROM PETER BELL

The verse-narrative of *Peter Bell*, originally written in 1798, was not published till 1819. The three stanzas given here (ll. 131–45) explain the fundamental idea of its composition, defined in the dedication to Southey as 'a belief that the Imagination not only does not require for its exercise the intervention of supernatural agency, but that, though such agency be excluded, the faculty may be called forth as imperiously and for kindred results of pleasure, by incidents, within the compass of poetic probability, in the humblest departments of daily life.' The whole poem contains many passages and phrases which distinguish it as the work of a great poet; but, although at the present day it is read with a fuller appreciation of its author's genius and his real intention, it must be owned that he imperilled his reputation by pushing his theory of the power of common-place incident on the imagination to an extreme point. His attitude to the critics who made the most of his insistence on trivial details and his baldness of phrase is expressed in the sonnet, 'A Book came forth of late, called PETER BELL,' modelled on Milton's 'Tetrachordon' sonnet and published in his *Miscellaneous Works*, 1820.

6. The allusion is to the hippogriff and magic ring which appear as supernatural elements in the *Orlando Furioso* of Ariosto. Similar features are found in other romantic narratives: cf. the magic horse and ring in Chaucer's *Squire's Tale*.

LUCY

'Composed in the Hartz Forest' in 1799; published in 1800; classified among Poems of the Imagination (No. x). This beautiful exposition of the power of Nature to mould the receptive mind in her likeness should be compared with the address to Dorothy Wordsworth in ll. 119 sqq. of *Tintern Abbey* (p. 9 above). The other poems of the same period, viz. 'She dwelt among the untrodden ways,' 'Strange fits of passion have I known,' and 'I travelled among unknown men' (Poems of the Affections, Nos. VII–IX), also deal with Lucy, apparently an ideal figure created by Wordsworth.

10. **In earth and heaven**] Cf. the Wanderer's speech in *Excursion*, IX, 265–70, referring to the village pastor's two sons:

> For every genial power of heaven and earth,
> Through all the seasons of the changeful year,
> Obsequiously doth take upon herself
> To labour for them.

13. **as the fawn**] Cf. *Tintern Abbey*, 68, 69 (p. 7 above). Wordsworth himself, in attaining 'the silence and the calm' referred to in l. 17, had lost the animal spirits of his earlier days. Here the two qualities are combined: the healing calm of Nature lends its thoughtful cast to natural gaiety of disposition without repressing it. See also the lines *To Louisa*, 3–6:

> Why should I fear to say
> That, nymph-like, she is fleet and strong,
> And down the rocks can leap along
> Like rivulets in May?

39. **She died**] Cf. 'She dwelt among the untrodden ways,' 9-12:

> She lived unknown, and few could know
> When Lucy ceased to be;
> But she is in her grave, and, oh,
> The difference to me.

SELECTIONS FROM MICHAEL

Michael, a pastoral poem, consisting of 482 lines, was written in the autumn and early winter of 1800 at Dove cottage, Town-end, Grasmere, and published at the end of the year. Classified among Poems founded on the Affections (No. XXXII). The selections given here are ll. 40–139, 194–203, 448–82. Wordsworth founded the narrative upon the story of a family to whom Dove cottage had belonged many years before. He connected its main incidents with the remains of a ruined sheep-fold in the valley of Greenhead gill, which descends from Rydal fell to the Easedale beck about a mile and a half beyond Dove cottage, on the road to Keswick. The first selection gives the account of the *dramatis personae*, the old shepherd, his wife and their son. As the son grew up, he became his father's 'comfort and his daily hope.' But, when the boy was eighteen, Michael was called upon to discharge the debts of a nephew for whom he had stood surety. Unwilling to sell his lands and deprive Luke of his succession, he determined to send him to a prosperous tradesman of his kindred, in whose employment he would be able to retrieve this loss. The tradesman consented to receive the boy, and preparations were made for his departure. The night before he left home, his father took him to the heap of stones which had been collected to build a sheep-fold, and, reminding him of the love which existed between them and bound them to their simple forefathers, the rustic dwellers in the same spot, bade him lay the corner-stone as a covenant between them, the memory of which would recall the life his ancestors had lived and stand as a shield against the temptations of the world outside his native valleys. The boy consented with a full heart, but temptation was too strong for him: he fell into dissolute courses and disgrace, and Michael and his wife were left in their lonely old age. The conclusion of the story is given in the third selection.

Simple as the narrative is, 'unenriched with strange events' and told in the plainest language, it occupies a place of great importance in Wordsworth's poetical work. He tells us that

> it was the first
> Of those domestic tales that spake to me
> Of shepherds, dwellers in the valleys, men
> Whom I already loved; not verily
> For their own sakes, but for the fields and hills
> Which were their occupation and abode.

Gradually this sympathy with the living occupants of the scenes which he loved took a more active shape and broadened into love of man and enthusiasm for the nobility of the simple type of character which, as in the case of Michael, had Nature for its only teacher. Earlier poems, such as *Ruth*, had expressed this feeling; but *Michael* is taken directly from Wordsworth's immediate surroundings at the time of writing and reproduces them and the kinship between them and their inhabitants with a peculiar natural skill. Matthew Arnold gave it special prominence among the poems which illustrate Wordsworth's unique power, 'the successful balance....of profound truth of subject with profound truth of execution.' No one who recognises the function of poetry to reflect and interpret life can fail to see that the unadorned style of *Michael* bears the closest relation possible to the bareness of mountain solitudes and the frugal life of those who earn their scanty and hard-won living among them. If Wordsworth's language is austerely simple and may even at times be bald, 'it is,' as Matthew Arnold says, 'bald as the bare mountain-tops are bald, with a baldness which is full of grandeur,' and its freedom from luxuries of phrase is at one with the necessary sacrifice of superfluous comfort 'in huts where poor men lie.' To quote Arnold again, 'Nature herself seems to take the pen out of his hand, and to write for him with her own bare, sheer, penetrating power.'

I. The Evening Star

1. **the forest-side**] A forest is not necessarily a woodland district, but implies, in the legal sense of the word, an unenclosed tract of land used for purposes of hunting, like the forest of Dartmoor. The word is still given to ranges of bare hills in various parts of the British isles, e.g. Macclesfield forest, Radnor forest and the mountains known as the Fforest fawr (i.e. great forest) which divide Breconshire from Glamorgan and Carmarthenshire.

20. **many thousand mists**] Cf. this description of the shepherd's life with the longer passage in *The Prelude*, VIII, 223-93, especially the striking passage in ll. 262-75:

> When up the lonely brooks on rainy days
> Angling I went, or trod the trackless hills
> By mists bewildered, suddenly mine eyes
> Have glanced upon him distant a few steps,
> In size a giant, stalking through the fog,
> His sheep like Greenland bears; or, as he stepped
> Beyond the boundary line of some hill-shadow,
> His form hath flashed upon me, glorified

By the deep radiance of the setting sun:
Or him have I described in distant sky,
A solitary object and sublime,
Above all height! like an aerial cross
Stationed alone upon a spiry rock
Of the Chartreuse, for worship.

95. Easedale is the valley north-west of Grasmere. There is an elaborate description of it in De Quincey's essay, *Early Memorials of Grasmere*. Dunmail-raise is one of the hills north of Grasmere, over the shoulder of which the high-road from Ambleside to Keswick passes. Wordsworth notes that the cottage known as the 'Evening Star' was not actually Dove cottage, but 'another on the same side of the valley, more to the north.' A house called Forest Side (see note on l. 1 above) stands at the point indicated, near the foot of Greenhead gill.

II. The Shepherd and his Son

9. A line characteristic of Wordsworth at his best, creating magical effects by the use of the simplest words. All that Michael had learned to love in Nature was endeared to him still more by its association with human ties.

III. The Unfinished Sheep-Fold

1. The selection begins at the point where the story of Luke's disgrace has been told. The unchanging beauties of Nature remain, as the old man pursues his daily occupations (ll. 8 sqq.), and with them remain the indelible memories of the past life with his son and the associations which it had given to his natural surroundings. Thus, amid disappointment, the strength of love with its recollections becomes a source of comfort and fortitude.

19. Matthew Arnold cites this line as 'the right sort of verse to choose from Wordsworth, if we are to seize his true and most characteristic form of expression...There is nothing subtle in it, no heightening, no study of poetic style, strictly so called, at all; yet it is expression of the highest and most truly expressive kind.' This criticism is perhaps exaggerated, as regards its first part: Wordsworth's most characteristic form of expression is found in lines like l. 9 in the selected passage immediately preceding this, in which we find a perfect illustration of Coleridge's remark (*Biog. Literaria*, ed. Ashe, p. 232) that, in the exercise of imaginative power, 'he does indeed to all thoughts and to all objects

add the gleam,
The light that never was on sea or land,
The consecration, and the poet's dream.'

The present line seems to fall short of this highest attainment, in that it lacks the full charm of imagination. But, if it fails to stimulate in the same degree, the truth of the second part of Arnold's statement is unchanged. It expresses simply and completely the mental attitude of Michael in words which no heightening of phrase could improve, and therefore has a peculiarly dramatic value and imaginative power of its own.

TO JOANNA

The second poem of the series entitled Poems on the naming of places. Joanna Hutchinson was a younger sister of Mary Hutchinson, who became Wordsworth's wife in 1802. Dorothy Wordsworth (*Journals*, I, 46) notes on 23 Aug. 1800: 'Wm. read *Peter Bell* and the poem of *Joanna*, beside the Rothay by the roadside'; which fixes the approximate date of composition. It was published in 1800. Wordsworth's preliminary note says: 'The effect of her laugh is an extravagance; though the effect of the reverberation of voices in some parts of the mountains is very striking. There is, in the "Excursion", an allusion to the bleat of a lamb thus re-echoed, and described without any exaggeration, as I heard it, on the side of Stickle-Tarn, from the precipice that stretches on to Langdale Pikes.' See *The Excursion*, IV, 402-10, and cf. the echo of the raven's cry, *ibid.* IV, 1176–87 (selection VII, 23 sqq., p. 102 above), the origin of which appears from Dorothy Wordsworth's journal (I, 44) for 27 July, 1800. 'It called out, and the dome of the sky seemed to echo the sound. It called again and again as it flew onwards, and the mountains gave back the sound, seeming as if from their centre; a musical bell-like answering to the bird's hoarse voice.' Dorothy was reminded of this poem at Cartland crags, Lanark, 21 Aug. 1803 (*ibid.* I, 198): 'I wish Joanna had been there to laugh, for the echo is an excellent laughter, and would have almost made her believe that it was a true story which William has told of her and the mountains.'

13. **two long years**] In August, 1800, William and Dorothy Wordsworth had been settled at Dove cottage, Grasmere, for little more than eight months. The incident related in the poem appears to be an imaginary combination of Joanna's laughter with the effect of mountain echoes.

19. **those lofty firs**] The fir-grove called by the Wordsworths John's grove after their brother John, and described in the lines 'When to the attractions of the busy world,' composed about this time.

28. **a Runic Priest**] Wordsworth notes: 'In Cumberland and Westmorland are several Inscriptions, upon the native rock, which, from the wasting of time, and the rudeness of the workmanship, have been mistaken for Runic. They are without doubt Roman.' Runes (from old Norse *rún*, a whisper) are the characters, consisting of combinations of straight lines, used in Scandinavian and certain old English inscriptions, as upon the famous Ruthwell cross in Dumfriesshire, where runic characters and Latin inscriptions with the ordinary lettering appear upon the same work of art. The word 'rune' was applied to such characters in after times because of their supposed mysterious

significance; but their actual origin was the use of tally-sticks by Baltic merchants, who notched their memoranda upon the wood in the form best suited to its grain. Wordsworth's phrase must be taken to mean 'a heathen priest,' who expresses his mysterious meaning in runes.

31. **the Rotha**] Or Rothay, a stream which, rising in Silver How, N.W. of Grasmere, expands into the lakes of Grasmere and Rydal, and, after joining the Brathay, falls into Windermere at its north end. Cf. Matthew Arnold, *Memorial Verses*:

> Keep fresh the grass upon his grave,
> O Rotha, with thy living wave!
> Sing him thy best! for few or none
> Hears thy voice right, now he is gone.

32. **those dear immunities of heart**] Wordsworth's answer was dictated by the mischievous wish to mystify the vicar, tempered by real affection for him. The mingled sentiment produced an irresponsible feeling of welcome gaiety which coloured Wordsworth's account of the incident. Immunity=freedom from responsibility.

56. **Helm–crag**] 'On Helm-crag, that impressive single mountain at the head of the Vale of Grasmere, is a rock which from most points of view bears a striking resemblance to an old Woman cowering. Close by this rock is one of those fissures or caverns, which in the language of the country are called dungeons.' Helm-crag stands at the foot of the pass between Grasmere and Thirlmere, on the left-hand of the road from Ambleside to Keswick. The rocks, changing in shape as the traveller advances, seem from certain points to form two figures, known as the Astrologer and thd Old woman,

> Dread pair that, spite of wind and weather,
> Shall sit upon Helm-crag together.
>
> (*The Waggoner*, I, 178, 179.)

56–65. The echo is taken up by the hills south of Helm-crag. From Loughrigg, which stands south of Grasmere and

Rydal waters, it travels north to Fairfield, a mountain S.W. of Helvellyn, and thence is carried to Helvellyn and across the vale of Keswick to Skiddaw. From this point it is taken southwards again to Glaramara, the highest of the Borrowdale fells at the head of Derwentwater, and finally to the mountains at the head of the Kirkstone pass, on the road from Windermere to Ullswater. Cf. *The Excursion*, IV, 1181-7 (selection VII, ll. 26–32, p. 102 above). Coleridge (*Biog. Literaria*, ed. Ashe, p. 200), referring to the echo in *Joanna* as an instance of a diction peculiarly Wordsworth's own, calls the passage a 'noble imitation of Drayton (if it was not rather a coincidence).' In Drayton's *Poly-olbion*, XXX, 155-64, the song of Copeland forest, the tract of fells between Ennerdale and Wastwater, is echoed by the neighbouring mountains and streams.

TO THE CUCKOO

Begun at Grasmere, 23 March, 1802 (Dorothy Wordsworth, *Journals*, I, 103). Published 1807: classified with Poems of the Imagination (No. II). For the influence of the cuckoo's song upon the imagination, cf. *The Solitary Reaper*, 13–16, and *Excursion*, selection II, 29, 30 (pp. 34, 95 above) and the beautiful stanzas by Matthew Arnold, *Thyrsis*, 51–76.

4. **a wandering Voice**] The cuckoo's voice in its season is heard everywhere, but the bird itself is seldom seen.

25–32. Cf. the description of the splendour of earth as it appears to the child's imagination in *Intimations of Immortality*, 4, 5 (p. 43 above). The cuckoo's song by the power of association brings back the glory of the earth and transfigures 'the light of common day.'

MY HEART LEAPS UP WHEN I BEHOLD

Written at Town-end, Grasmere, in 1802. Dorothy Wordsworth, *Journals*, I, 104, notes its composition on Friday, [26] March, 1802; and (*ibid.* I, 122) says that Wordsworth, on the night of 14 May, was 'haunted with altering *The Rainbow*.' It was published in *Poems*, 1807, and was afterwards placed first among the series of Poems referring to the period of Childhood. The last three lines were used as the motto of the ode on *Intimations of Immortality*, a poem which enlarges upon the idea contained in them.

9. **natural piety**] Devotion, like that of a child to a parent, to Nature, which, pursued unswervingly, becomes an animating and sustaining influence to the soul. It is the gradual decay of this 'natural piety,' the failure to recognise in manhood the 'vision splendid' which the child sees in the commonest natural objects, that Wordsworth laments in *Intimations of Immortality*.

COMPOSED UPON WESTMINSTER BRIDGE

'Written on the roof of a coach, on my way to France' (Wordsworth). The true date, according to Dorothy Wordsworth (*Journals*, I, 144, 145), was 31 July, 1802, about 5·30 or 6·30 A.M. The same scene, on a Sunday evening, inspired in more recent times the first of W. E. Henley's *London Voluntaries*, in which the sight of 'the silent River, ranging tide-mark high' forms part of the setting of a poem filled with the music of the bells of St Margaret's. The sonnet was published in 1807, and was arranged later as No. XXXVI of Miscellaneous sonnets, Part II.

IT IS A BEAUTEOUS EVENING, CALM AND FREE

'This was composed on the beach near Calais, in the autumn of 1802' (Wordsworth)—strictly speaking, in August, 1802, when Wordsworth and his sister spent four weeks at Calais. Published in *Poems*, 1807: afterwards No. xxx of Misc. sonnets, Part I.

2. **a Nun]** The peace and quietness of a nun's life are often alluded to by Wordsworth: see, e.g., the sonnet 'Nuns fret not at their convent's narrow room,' and the somewhat sentimental *Ecclesiastical Sonnets*, I, xxii, which forms a striking contrast to No. xx of the same series.

9–14. Cf. *Tintern Abbey*, 110–59, and see note, p. 112 above. The idea which links these six lines to those that precede them is that, just as the voice of the sea is ever-present, though we are fully conscious of it only when we listen, so, even in moments least touched by seriousness, the naturally reverent soul retains its sub-conscious sense of the divine presence. Cf. *Excursion*, IV, 1147–50:

Here you stand,
Adore, and worship, when you know it not;
Pious beyond the intention of your thought;
Devout above the meaning of your will.

TO TOUSSAINT L'OUVERTURE

Probably composed at Calais in August, 1802. Printed in *The Morning Post*, 2 Feb. 1803. Published in *Poems*, 1807: classified later among Poems dedicated to National Independence and Liberty (Part I, No. VIII). Toussaint, born in 1743, was a negro slave who, after the abolishment of slavery in San Domingo by the national convention, became governor and dictator of the whole island, establishing his rule over the Spanish as well as the French part of the colony. His independent policy, although he professed a loyalty to France which was never actually disproved, was hostile to Napoleon's ideals. In 1801 the first consul sent his brother-in-law, general Leclerc, at the head of an expedition to San Domingo, which, in pursuance of secret instructions, suppressed the negro domination. Toussaint was brought to France in June, 1802, and imprisoned, first in the Temple at Paris, and afterwards at the fort of Joux in the Jura, where he died in 1803.

4. **earless**] Beyond the reach of sound or of human hearing. The 'ear' of a prison is its means of communication with the outer world: at Syracuse is the old quarry, known as Dionysius' ear, because the polished grooves in its limestone sides were supposed to have been made in order that the tyrant might listen to the groans of the persons imprisoned in it. Cf. also the 'lug' or ear through which Scott, in *The Fortunes of Nigel*, makes James I overhear the talk of prisoners in one of the cells of the tower of London.

9–15. Nature and man's noblest emotions, inspired by Nature, are on the side of the victim of tyranny.

LONDON, 1802

Composed during Wordsworth's stay in London, Sept. 1802. Published in *Poems*, 1807: classified later among Poems dedicated to National Independence and Liberty (Part I, No. XIV). The love of Milton had a profound effect upon Wordsworth's poetic style, which is constantly exemplified in *The Prelude*, *The Excursion*, and the sonnets. Even more important than this was his admiration of Milton as the champion of English liberty. De Quincey, in his essay on Wordsworth, enlarges upon the extraordinary likeness to Wordsworth of the Portrait of Milton in Richardson's volume of notes on *Paradise Lost*—'a likeness nearly perfect...better by much than any which I have since seen of those expressly painted for himself.'

4. **hall and bower]** The hall and bower were the two living-rooms which composed the chief part of the English dwelling-house from very early times and continued to be the nucleus of the plan of the larger houses until the middle of the seventeenth century. The hall was the common room of the household, while the bower was the private room of the master of the house and the withdrawing-room of the ladies. In process of time, the latter word was specially applied to a room used by the ladies of the household; and in this passage 'hall and bower' are used as symbols of the conditions under which masculine and feminine virtues have grown up in England. For the division of the house into hall and bower cf. Chaucer, *Cant. Tales*, B 4022: 'Ful sooty was hir bour, and eek hir halle.'

COMPOSED AFTER A JOURNEY ACROSS THE HAMBLETON HILLS

'Composed 4th October, 1802,...on a day memorable to me—the day of my marriage.' Published 1807: classified among Misc. sonnets, Part II, No. XI. Wordsworth was married to Mary Hutchinson at Brompton-in-Pickering-lythe, near Scarborough: they travelled the same day, by way of Helmsley, Rievaulx and Thirsk, to Leeming, between Thirsk and Bedale. Dorothy Wordsworth, who accompanied them, describes (*Journals*, I, 150, 151) the journey in words which form a commentary on the sonnet: she and her brother had taken the reverse route on 15 July previously (*ibid.* I, 142, 143). 'Far far off from us, in the western sky, we saw shapes of castles, ruins among groves, a great spreading wood, rocks, and single trees, a minster with its tower unusually distinct, minarets in another quarter and a round Grecian temple also; the colours of the sky of a bright grey, and the forms of a sober grey, with a dome. As we descended the hill there was no distinct view, but of a great space; only near us we saw the wild (and as the people say) bottomless tarn in the hollow at the side of the hill. It seemed to be made visible to us only by its own light, for all the hill about us was dark.' The road from Helmsley to Thirsk, after ascending the steep bank above Rievaulx, runs along the top of the Hambledon hills and comes suddenly to the precipice of Whitestone cliff, from the edge of which there is a magnificent view of the vales of York and Mowbray, with the hills and moors of Wensleydale and Swaledale in the western distance. The road descends the face of the bank called Sutton brow, with the tarn called Gormire below it on the right hand, to the village of Sutton.

TO THE DAISY

Composed in the orchard at Town-end, 1802. Published in *Poems*, 1807. Classified among Poems of the Fancy (No. VII). Wordsworth prefixed to it a motto from George Wither, *The Shepherd's Hunting*, eclogue IV, 366–78, which forms a sufficient comment on the poem. In Wither's lines, Philarete (the lover of virtue) describes the lessons taught him by his Muse:

Her divine skill taught me this,
That from everything I saw
I could some invention draw,
And raise pleasure to her height
Through the meanest object's sight.
By the murmur of a spring,
Or the least bough's rusteling;
By a daisy whose leaves spread
Shut when Titan goes to bed,
Or a shady bush or tree,
She could more infuse in me
Than all Nature's beauties can
In some other wiser man.

In the third line, Wordsworth altered 'invention' to 'instruction,' and his version contains one or two other trifling variations.

1. Cf. *Tintern Abbey*, 72 sqq. (p. 7 above), for a more elaborate contrast between Wordsworth's earlier and later love of Nature.

17. **a morrice train]** Like a band of morris dancers in fancy dresses. For the morris, i.e. Moorish, dance see Milton, *Comus*, 116:

> The sounds and seas, with all their finny drove,
> Now to the moon in wavering morrice move.

25. **mews]** Enclosures. A mew is properly a cage for hawks.

32. **The Poet's darling]** Cf. Chaucer's praise of the daisy, *Legend of Good Women*, prologue B, 180–211, 'the emperice and flour of floures alle.'

44. **Some apprehension]** Cf. the last two lines of *Intimations of Immortality*, p. 51 above.

THE GREEN LINNET

Composed at Grasmere, 1803, in the orchard at Town-end, Wordsworth's favourite place for composition. Published in *Poems*, 1807. Classified among Poems of the Fancy (No. IX). This bird-poem forms a suitable pendant to the preceding flower-poem; but it expresses Wordsworth's purely objective delight in the fluttering and song of the linnet, while *To the Daisy* is devoted more exclusively to the subjective emotions which the sight of the flower calls forth.

25. **yon tuft]** Cf. 'orchard-tufts' in *Tintern Abbey*, II (p. 5 above).

YEW-TREES

Written at Grasmere, 1803. Published in the collected edition of the poems, 1815. Classified among Poems of the Imagination (No. V).

1. **Lorton Vale]** The valley down which the Cocker flows to join the Derwent from the northern end of Crummock water. The yew referred to is at High Lorton, a village on the road from Keswick to Cockermouth.

4. **weapons**] Shafts for bows.

5. **Umfraville or Percy**] Gilbert Umfraville, earl of Angus (1310–81), who fought against the Scots at Neville's cross in 1346, became lord of Cockermouth by his marriage with the heiress Maud Lucy. On his death, his widow married Henry Percy, first earl of Northumberland (1342-1408): they had no children, and the lordship or honour of Cockermouth passed to the heirs of the earl of Northumberland's first marriage, who bore the arms of Percy quartered with those of Lucy. The chief possessions of the Umfravilles and Percys lay in Northumberland, where their tenants formed a barrier to Scottish inroads.

14. These yews are close to Seathwaite, at the head of Borrowdale, the valley at the south end of Derwentwater. The lines (13–33) describing these trees, with so magnificent an employment of personification, are cited by Coleridge (*Biog. Literaria*, ed. Ashe, pp. 232, 233) as a striking instance of Wordsworth's imaginative power; in which 'he stands nearest of all modern writers to Shakespeare and Milton; and yet in a kind perfectly unborrowed and his own.'

18. **inveterately**] Obstinately from long habit.

19, 20. Their appearance awakens fantastic imaginings and raises apprehensions in those whose spirits are not initiated to their solemnity. Wordsworth, *Prelude*, VIII, 379, 380, speaks of the romantic influence of yew-trees upon the awakening imagination which is beginning to express itself in poetry:

> the yew-tree had its ghost,
> That took his station there for ornament.

For maturer minds the yew has a deeper and less fantastic significance.

22. **the pining umbrage**] The dying foliage. 'Umbrage,' the shadow given by the foliage, is here expressively used for the foliage itself.

32. **the mountain flood**] The Derwent, which has its source in the fells immediately S.W. of Glaramara (see note on ll. 56-65, pp. 120, 121 above).

WHO FANCIED WHAT A PRETTY SIGHT

Written at Grasmere, 1803. Published in *Poems*, 1807. Classified among Poems of the Fancy (No. XIV). Of this and 'I wandered lonely as a cloud' (p. 38 above) Wordsworth wrote to lady Beaumont, 21 May, 1807: 'I am sure that whoever is much pleased with either of these quiet and tender delineations must be fitted to walk through the recesses of my poetry with delight and will there recognise, at every turn, something or other in which and over which, it has that property and right which knowledge and love confer' (*Memorials of Coleorton*, II, 16). A somewhat similar subject, of which there is a record in Dorothy Wordsworth's journal for 24 April, 1802 (I, 113), prompted *The Primrose of the Rock*, written in 1831:

A Rock there is whose homely front
  The passing traveller slights;
Yet there the glow-worms hang their lamps,
  Like stars, at various heights;
And one coy Primrose to that Rock
  The vernal breeze invites.

THE SOLITARY REAPER

No. IX of the series classified as *Memorials of a Tour in Scotland*, 1803, the tour described with admirable fulness and picturesqueness in Dorothy Wordsworth's *Journals*, who (II, 118, 119) quotes the poem in connexion with their visit to Loch Voil, Perthshire, 13 Sept. 1803. It was suggested, however, as both she and Wordsworth point out, less by their immediate surroundings than by 'a beautiful sentence in Thomas Wilkinson's *Tour in Scotland*.' In this respect, it differs from the three companion poems in the same series, which were directly suggested by incidents of the journey, viz. *To a Highland Girl* (28 August),

Stepping Westward (11 Sept.), and *The Matron of Jedborough* (20 and 21 Sept.). It is, however, the most beautiful of them all, combining Wordsworth's simplicity and directness of language with the charm of imaginative phrase (see, e.g. ll. 15, 16) in a degree which he nowhere surpassed. Most of the poems of the series were composed after the events which they recall. The greater number were published in 1807.

11. **some shady haunt**] An oasis in the desert.

16. **the farthest Hebrides**] The effect of this beautiful couplet may be compared with that of the opening lines of Andrew Marvell's *Song of the Emigrants in Bermuda*:

> Where the remote Bermudas ride
> In the ocean's bosom unespied,
> From a small boat that row'd along
> The listening winds received this song.

20. **battles long ago**] Wordsworth was thinking of the abundance of Scottish ballad-poetry dealing with past history, the plaintive spirit of which is rendered, e.g., by Burns' *Lament for Culloden* and in the refrain, 'The Flowers of the Forest are a' wede away,' of Jane Elliott's *Lament for Flodden.* Wordsworth's lines, with their burden of memory, recall, perhaps unintentionally, passages in Ford's *The Lover's Melancholy,* IV, 2:

> Sigh out a lamentable tale of things
> Done long ago, and ill done;

and IV, 3:

> Parthenophil is lost, and I would see him;
> For he is like to something I remember
> A great while since, a long, long time ago.

32. This line was taken directly from Thomas Wilkinson's account of the song of a solitary reaper in Ayrshire, in his *Tour to the British Mountains,* which Wordsworth saw in MS. It was not published till 1824.

YARROW UNVISITED

No. XIII of the same series, published in 1807. Wordsworth's refusal to visit Yarrow, 18 Sept. 1803, is recorded by Dorothy Wordsworth, *Journals*, II, 131–3, where the text of the poem is also given. Yarrow water rises among the hills which form the watershed between the Tweed and Clyde, and, flowing through the two lakes known as the Loch of the Lowes and St Mary's loch, joins Ettrick water two miles above Selkirk and enters the Tweed between Selkirk and Abbotsford. The Scottish ballad which inspired this beautiful poem was William Hamilton of Bangour's (d. 1754) *The Braes of Yarrow*:

Busk ye, busk ye, my bonny, bonny Bride,
Busk ye, busk ye, my winsome Marrow!

1–4. The tour was begun on 14 August. The Wordsworths and Coleridge travelled into Scotland by way of Carlisle and Dumfries, entered the Clyde valley near Lanark on 20 August and arrived at Glasgow on the 22nd. From Glasgow they went to Loch Lomond and Loch Katrine. Coleridge left them on 29 August at Arrochar on Loch Long, and the two Wordsworths pursued their journey into the western Highlands as far as Ballachulish at the head of Loch Linnhe. Here they turned eastwards through Glencoe, and down Strath Tay as far as Dunkeld. From this point they made a digression westwards, and, after visiting Loch Katrine and Loch Lomond again, were at Stirling on 14 Sept. They slept at Falkirk on the 14th, Edinburgh on the 15th, Rosslyn on the 16th, visited Scott at Lasswade on the 17th, slept at Peebles, and on the 18th came down the Tweed valley from Peebles to Clovenfords near Galashiels. After another week, most of which was spent in Scott's company at Melrose, Jedburgh and Hawick, they returned to Grasmere on 25 Sept. It is worth notice that this tour was undertaken before Scott's *Lady of the Lake* had given the Scottish lakes their fame and popularity, in regions then rarely visited by English tourists.

6. *Marrow*] A friend or companion. The quotation is from Hamilton's ballad: see introductory note.

8. **Braes**] Hill-sides.

17. Gala water has its source in the Moorfoot hills, N.E. of Peebles, and enters the Tweed south of Galashiels, between Abbotsford and Melrose. Leader water rises in the Lammermuir hills and joins the Tweed below Melrose. 'Haughs' are flat pastures beside a river.

19. **Dryborough**] The abbey of Dryburgh in Berwickshire, famous as the burial-place of Scott and otherwise of great interest as preserving a large portion of its monastic buildings in addition to the remains of its church, is on the left bank of the Tweed between Melrose and Kelso. It was founded for Premonstratensian canons in 1150, the first occupants being a colony of canons from Alnwick abbey in Northumberland. The situation, hidden in trees on a 'haugh' above a ford of the river, which is here of considerable breadth, running among woods and cliffs of red sandstone and forming a bold curve round the promontory on which the abbey stands, is remarkable for its peaceful beauty.

chiming Tweed] Not less beautiful than this is the famous passage in Lockhart's *Life of Scott*, ch. lxxxiii, describing Sir Walter's death, twenty-nine years, all but a day, after Wordsworth's visit to Dryburgh (20 Sept. 1803): 'It was a beautiful day—so warm that every window was wide open—and so perfectly still, that the sound of all others most delicious to his ear, the gentle ripple of the Tweed over its pebbles, was distinctly audible as we knelt around the bed, and his eldest son kissed and closed his eyes.'

20. **lintwhites**] Linnets.

21. **Tiviot-dale**] The Teviot rises on the borders of Roxburghshire and Dumfriesshire and, flowing past Hawick, joins the Tweed on its right bank, just above Kelso bridge.

33. **holms**] Flat meadows by water: cf. 'haughs,' l. 17 above.

43. **still St Mary's Lake]** Described by Scott, *Marmion*, introd. to canto II:

> Oft in my mind such thoughts awake,
> By lone Saint Mary's silent lake;
> Thou know'st it well,—nor fen, nor sedge,
> Pollute the pure lake's crystal edge;
> Abrupt and sheer, the mountains sink
> At once upon the level brink;
> And just a trace of silver sand
> Marks where the water meets the land.
> Far in the mirror, bright and blue,
> Each hill's huge outline you may view;
> Shaggy with heath, but lonely bare,
> Nor tree, nor bush, nor brake is there,
> Save where, of land, yon slender line
> Bears thwart the lake the scatter'd pine.

The lake, 'among the soft and melancholy wildernesses where Yarrow creeps from her fountains' (Lockhart, *Life of Scott*, ch. xvi), takes its name from the ruined church of St Mary, 'Mary's Chapel of the Lowes,' which stands on its eastern side. Scott notes: 'In the winter, it is still frequented by flights of wild swans,' and proceeds to quote Wordsworth's lines from memory.

SHE WAS A PHANTOM OF DELIGHT

Written at Grasmere, 1804. Published 1807. Classified among Poems of the Imagination (No. VIII). Wordsworth says: 'The germ of this poem was four lines composed as a part of the verses on the Highland Girl. Though beginning in this way, it was written from my heart, as is sufficiently obvious.' The poem appears to have reached its present form shortly after

Wordsworth's marriage (see note on p. 125 above). *To a Highland Girl* contains the following lines:

> But, O fair Creature! in the light
> Of common day, so heavenly bright,
> I bless thee, Vision as thou art,
> I bless thee with a human heart.
> *   *   *   *   *   *   *
> For never saw I mien, or face,
> In which more plainly I could trace
> Benignity and home-bred sense
> Ripening in perfect innocence.

The stanzas should be compared with *Prelude*, XIV, 266–75, in which, at the conclusion of lines addressed to his sister, Wordsworth pays a tribute to the influence of his wife (see ll. 35-44, p. 90 above).

22. **The very pulse of the machine**] The image is bold and not very graceful. What Wordsworth means is that he discerns the animating spirit which directs his wife in the common tasks of daily life. Such tasks, mechanical in themselves are ennobled by a conscious and contented obedience to duty, the ' stern Daughter of the Voice of God.'

I WANDERED LONELY AS A CLOUD

Wordsworth dated this poem, published in 1807 (without the second stanza) and classified afterwards among Poems of the Imagination (No. XII), as composed in 1804. His note is: ' Written at Town-end, Grasmere. The Daffodils grew and still grow on the margin of Ullswater, and probably may be seen to this day as beautiful in the month of March, nodding their golden heads beside the dancing and foaming waves.' Dorothy Wordsworth (*Journals*, I, 106) shews that the idea of the stanzas must have taken root as early as 15 April, 1802, when she and her brother were walking along the left bank of Ullswater.

21. **that inward eye**] See note on *Tintern Abbey*, 47 (p. 110 above). Coleridge (*Biog. Literaria*, ed. Ashe, p. 221) thought that ll. 23, 24, following upon this description of the association of visual images with the memory, had an effect of bathos, and cited the passage as a case in which there was 'a disproportion of thought to the circumstance and occasion,' adding 'This, by-the-by, is a fault of which none but a man of genius is capable.' Wordsworth attributed the suggestion of ll. 21, 22, 'the two best lines' in the poem, to his wife.

ODE TO DUTY

Written in 1805. Published 1807. Classified among Poems of Sentiment and Reflection (No. xx). 'This ode is on the model of Gray's Ode to Adversity, which is copied from Horace's Ode to Fortune' (i.e. Horace, *Carm.* I, xxxv). Wordsworth prefixed a Latin motto to the ode: 'Jam non consilio bonus, sed more eò perductus, ut non tantum rectè facere possim, sed nisi rectè facere non possim,' i.e. 'Good no longer of deliberate intent, but brought by the guidance of habit to such a point, that not only can I act rightly, but cannot act otherwise than rightly.'

1. The opening directly recalls the first line of Gray's ode, which addresses Adversity as 'Daughter of Jove, relentless power.' Duty is the offspring of conscience, the voice of God speaking to man. Wordsworth (*Excursion*, IV, 226) speaks of the reverence due to conscience 'as God's most intimate presence in the soul.'

3. **a light to guide**] Cf. Ps. cxix, 105. The same psalm provides several parallels to the first stanza of this ode: cf., e.g., ll. 5, 6 with *v.* 107, and l. 7 with *vv.* 113, 176.

19, 20. Love and joy are strengthened and purified by duty. Love leaves vain desires for steady and permanent objects: joy finds its security in its consciousness of right motive.

28. **my trust**] i.e. in my own direction. He has tried to do what is right and resist casual inclinations, but, depending

upon his own counsel, has not always acted in harmony with duty.

33. **no disturbance of my soul**] Cf. *Laodamia*, 74, 75:

the Gods approve
The depth, and not the tumult, of the soul.

37. **unchartered**] Without the charter or privilege which duty confers.

38. **chance-desires**] The casual longings which tempt the soul to restlessness when in a condition of uncontrolled freedom. Devotion to duty (ll. 39, 40) controls the temptation to random fancies and gives the mind settled repose.

45-8. Outward nature and the solar system, in their unchanging obedience to law, preserve an eternal freshness and recuperative power which contrast with the wavering obedience of man. Cf. Ps. cxlviii, 6.

53. **lowly wise**] Wise with humility. The phrase is borrowed from Milton, *P.L.* VIII, 173.

55. **The confidence of reason**] The ultimate conviction of the blessedness of obedience to duty lies in the acquiescence of the human reason to her commands. Without this intellectual assent such obedience, if it were actually possible, would be purely mechanical, and consciousness of love and joy (ll. 19, 20) would be absent. In *The Happy Warrior*, 27, reason is the law upon which Wordsworth's ideal character, a model of obedience to duty, relies:

—'Tis he whose law is reason; who depends
Upon that law as on the best of friends.

COMPOSED BY THE SIDE OF GRASMERE LAKE

Wordsworth added the date 1806 to the title of this sonnet. It was published in 1819, and was afterwards classified among Poems dedicated to National Independence and Liberty (Part II, No. V), where it follows the sonnet 'High deeds, O Germans, are to come from you,' written in February, 1807.

8. **incessant wars**] 1806 was the year of the victory of Napoleon over Prussia at Jena, followed by his winter campaign against Russia.

9–11. Is it actually a reflection, or is it a vision of the fires in the centre of the earth?

12. **Great Pan**] The personification of Nature. Cf. the sonnet (1809) beginning

> O'er the wide earth, on mountain and on plain,
> Dwells in the affections and the soul of man
> A Godhead, like the universal PAN.

See also Milton, *P.L.* IV, 266: 'Universal Pan.'

the reeds] The nymph Syrinx, pursued by Pan, was changed into a reed, out of which he made his pipe, the musical instrument with which he is represented. Cf. Elizabeth Barrett Browning's poem:

> What was he doing, the great god Pan,
> Down in the reeds by the river?

WITH SHIPS THE SEA WAS SPRINKLED

Dated by Wordsworth 1806. Published 1807. Classified among Miscellaneous sonnets (I, xxxii), where it follows the kindred sonnet, 'Where lies the Land to which yon Ship must go?' The sonnet is analysed in a letter from Wordsworth to lady Beaumont, written at Coleorton, 21 May, 1807 (*Memorials of Coleorton*, II, 12 sqq.), in which he defines its point as the selection of a single object from a crowd of similar things, and instances Milton's

> Hesperus, that led
> The starry host, rode brightest

(*Par. Lost*, IV, 605, 606) as an example of the influence of such single objects in calling forth the poetic faculty. Robert Bridges' poem, *A Passer-by*, has a somewhat similar subject to this and its companion sonnet:

> Whither, O splendid ship, thy white sails crowding,
> Leaning across the bosom of the urgent West,
> That fearest nor sea rising, nor sky clouding,
> Whither away, fair rover, and what thy quest?

ODE

INTIMATIONS OF IMMORTALITY FROM RECOLLECTIONS OF EARLY CHILDHOOD

This famous ode, published in 1807, appears to have been begun in June, 1802, to judge from entries in Dorothy Wordsworth's journals (see, e.g., 17 June, 1, 132). Wordsworth, who dated it 1803–6, says: 'Two years at least passed between the writing of the four first stanzas and the remaining part.' In his preface to the poem, he touches upon the 'particular feelings or *experiences* of my own mind on which the structure of the poem partly rests'—his incredulity during childhood of death as 'a state applicable to my own being,' his confidence of 'the indomitableness of the Spirit within me,' his early conviction that visible things had no external existence but were projections from his own 'immaterial nature,' and the growth of the opposite spirit of materialism in his later life, which made him look back to the illusions of childhood with the wistful desire to recover them. He further explains his view that the 'dream-like vividness and splendour which invest objects of sight in childhood' are 'presumptive evidence of a prior state of existence.' It is not advanced as a belief, but merely 'as an element in our instincts of immortality,' common to many religious creeds, familiar especially 'as an ingredient in Platonic philosophy,' and 'having sufficient foundation in humanity for authorising me to make for my purpose the best use of it I could as a poet.'

Briefly analysed, the argument of the poem is as follows. (1) Stt. I, II. Contrast between the beauty of Nature as seen in childhood, when everything is invested with a visionary, ideal charm, and the same sights in mature age, when the sense of beauty remains but the charm is gone. (2) Stt. III, IV develop the idea further. Amid the beauty of spring, the heart cannot but respond to the universal joy which is evident; but single natural objects remind it, even amid its joy, that something which childhood lent them has passed from them. (3) St. V traces the progress of life from birth to manhood and the gradual fading of the 'clouds of glory' which the soul brings from its former home. (4) In st. VI Wordsworth recognises the influence which Earth herself, offering pleasures and interests of her own, has upon this deterioration of the mind from its early ideals. This is exemplified in st. VII, where the overshadowing of the growing mind by the preoccupations and ambitions of ordinary life is traced, while its willingness to submit to the mastery of custom and the disillusion which this brings is lamented in st. VIII. (5) St. IX. Yet, in spite of this, man retains the power of reminiscence, which preserves his sense of the dream-like glory of his earliest ideas, and is an incentive to joy in later days. (6) In st. X the theme of stt. III, IV is renewed. The happiness which the spring morning awakens is not fruitless. If the fulness of the unalloyed happiness of the past cannot be restored, a quiet delight remains, and the years, with their teaching, have brought compensations. In the later part of st. X and in the concluding stanza, these are described. Sympathy with mankind has taken the place of a mere responsiveness to the magic beauty of natural surroundings, and Nature still claims her votary, exercising upon him a softening and sobering influence and deepening and enriching his contemplative faculty.

Wordsworth's picture of the progress of the mind from the turbulent hauntings of early youth to the philosophic calm of later life through disullusionment is an epitome of the experiences described in *The Prelude* and may be compared with the contrast of spirit recorded in *Tintern Abbey*. Here, however, he lays his stress upon the regret of early dreams for which mature wisdom cannot wholly compensate, and the most beautiful passages of the poem, the magnificent fifth stanza and the vision of the sea of immortality at the end of st. IX, are inspired by his sense of the source of such dreams in a state of pre-existence. The poem should be read side by side with Coleridge's *Dejection*, written in 1802, which, composed under the conviction of failing physical and mental powers, also treats the decay of pleasure in contemplating natural objects, but without a corresponding note of compensation for irreparable loss.

1–5. Cf. Henry Vaughan's beautiful lyric, *The Retreat*, which treats the same theme as this ode, especially ll. 11–14:

> When on some gilded cloud or flower
> My gazing soul would dwell an hour,
> And in those weaker glories spy
> Some shadows of eternity.

10. **The Rainbow**] Cf. the lines 'My heart leaps up when I behold,' p. 23 above.

14, 15. Cf. the sonnet *Composed by the side of Grasmere lake*, p. 42 above.

21. **the tabor's sound**] The tabor was a circular frame covered with parchment, something like a small kettle-drum, on which, suspended round his neck, the player beat with a stick with one hand, while with the other he held his pipe, to which the tabor formed an accompaniment. Cf. *Excursion*, II, 121–3:

> Tabor and pipe
> In purpose join to hasten or reprove
> The laggard Rustic.

25. Cf. *Tintern Abbey*, 76, 77, p. 8 above; and *Prelude*, VI, 626: 'The stationary blasts of waterfalls.'

28. **the fields of sleep**] This phrase has been variously interpreted as meaning the slumbering country-side or the west, which is the quarter of the sunset. The second alternative seems more probable; but possibly Wordsworth meant merely that

the wind was blowing so gently as to be hardly felt. Cf. his simile of 'sleeping flowers' for the winds when they are still, *The world is too much with us*, 7.

40. **coronal**] Garland, crown of flowers, worn upon festal occasions. Cf. *Yarrow Visited*, 69 (p. 62 above).

58. **a sleep and a forgetting**] I.e. a sleep between our previous and our present existences, in which the past is forgotten. Wordsworth in this stanza recalls the Platonic doctrine of a former existence in which the soul contemplates God and those ideal forms which are the archetypes of the forms of earth. According to Plato, all learning acquired in the earthly life is reminiscence, in which the soul learns to recognise the reflections of the ideals with which it had been conversant in its earlier home.

66. Cf. *Excursion*, IV, 83–6:

> Thou, who didst wrap the cloud
> Of infancy around us, that thyself,
> Therein, with our simplicity awhile
> Might'st hold, on earth, communion undisturbed.

67. **Shades of the prison-house**] Cf. the parable in Plato, *Republic*, VII, 1, where the soul in its state of ignorance is likened to men chained neck and foot in a cave from childhood, who see and hear only the shadows and echoes of the passing to and fro of people carrying various objects between them and the light of a distant fire at their backs. They take for realities the echoes and the shadows which the unseen fire throws on the walls of the cave in front of them.

71. **the east**] The dawn of life.

78. **in her own natural kind**] Which belong to her of nature and have no connexion with another state of existence.

82. **her Inmate Man**] The soul of man is imprisoned in its earthly form. So Waller, *On the Foregoing Divine Poems*, 13, calls the body 'the soul's dark cottage'; cf. *Excursion*, V, 589, 590: 'that dark house in which His soul is pent.'

103. **'humorous stage'**] Cf. Jaques' famous speech 'All the world's a stage' in Shakespeare, *As You Like It*, II, vii, 139–66.

The phrase is borrowed from Samuel Daniel's dedication of his *Musophilus* to Fulk Greville, and refers to the various humours or types of character which make up the drama of life. Man was supposed to be compounded of the four elements, each of which produced a special humour, and the preponderance of one over the others determined the complexion of his character.

107. **imitation**] The actor's business is to mimic real life.

108. **Thou**] This apostrophe, addressed to the child, recalls at its opening the hyperbolical fancies indulged so freely by the lyric poets of the seventeenth century, but rises, by the accumulation of images, to a sublimity which, in their bondage to ingenious plays of thought, they seldom attained.

111. **Thy heritage**] The philosopher is indifferent to earthly goods and is willing to resign his heritage for the sake of the pleasures of the mind. The child's heritage, on the other hand, is that reminiscence of a previous state which the philosopher would willingly retain. It is noteworthy that Wordsworth represents the child as possessing in the highest degree a gift which, in Plato's philosophy, comes with learning and advancing years. There is thus an important difference between the theory advanced in the ode and Plato's theory of pre-existence, which is, however, partially reconciled by the concluding stanzas.

113. **the eternal mind**] Cf. *Tintern Abbey*, 100–2, p. 8 above.

115, 116. Cf. the contrast in Matthew Arnold, *The Scholar-Gipsy*, between the unfettered life of the wandering scholar, with powers 'firm to their mark, not spent on other things,' and 'the sick fatigue, the languid doubt' of the ordinary human being:

O life unlike to ours!
Who fluctuate idly without term or scope,
Of whom each strives, nor knows for what he strives,
And each half lives a hundred different lives;
Who wait like thee, but not, like thee, in hope.

127. **custom]** Cf. Shelley. *The Revolt of Islam*, Dedication, 58, 59: 'the mortal chain of Custom.' This sense of the deadening effect of custom, habitual to poets who had come under the influence of revolutionary ideals, contrasts strongly with the devotion of the next generation, represented by Tennyson, to custom as the guardian of the settled form of life in which its poets found content. Cf. Tennyson, *In Memoriam*, XXIX:

> Use and Wont,
> That guard the portals of the house.

131–71. For this stanza cf. *Excursion*, IX, 36–44:

> Ah! why in age
> Do we revert so fondly to the walks
> Of childhood—but that there the Soul discerns
> The dear memorial footsteps unimpaired
> Of her own native vigour; thence can hear
> Reverberations; and a choral song
> Commingling with the incense that ascends,
> Undaunted, toward the imperishable heavens
> From her own lonely altar?

141. **those obstinate questionings]** The early stirrings of the philosophic temper. 'I was often unable,' writes Wordsworth, 'to think of external things as having external existence, and I communed with all that I saw as something not apart from, but inherent in, my own immaterial nature. Many times while going to school have I grasped at a wall or tree to recall myself form this abyss of idealism to the reality. At that time I was afraid of such processes. In later periods of life I have deplored, as we have all reason to do, a subjugation of an opposite character, as is expressed in the lines—

> Obstinate questionings
> Of sense and outward things,
> Fallings from us, vanishings; etc.'

162. **inland]** I.e. from the 'immortal sea' (l. 163) which, as it were, washes the child upon the shore of earth.

181. **the primal sympathy**] The fundamental sympathy between man and Nature of which man cannot be deprived, whatever may be the changes that come over his joy in natural beauty.

191. **more habitual**] If the glory of Nature has faded, yet, with advancing years, communion with her has become a habit and is less liable to distraction or sudden emotion.

192, 193. The early influence of streams upon Wordsworth is shewn in *Prelude*, I, 269–81, where he attributes some part of his love of Nature to the voice of the Derwent, familiar to him from his earliest childhood.

199. **Another race**] The meaning seems to be that sunset is not merely a thing of splendour and beauty: it becomes associated with thoughts of life and death, and the close of each day is, as it were, the close of a life, a race completed and crowned with a special reward to the individual soul which, identifying itself with Nature, receives daily fresh impressions and encouragement. Cf. the last stanza of *Composed upon an evening of extraordinary splendour and beauty*, pp. 65, 66 above.

THOUGHT OF A BRITON ON THE SUBJUGATION OF SWITZERLAND

Composed at Coleorton, Leices., in 1807, 'while pacing to and fro between the Hall of Coleorton, then rebuilding, and the principal Farm-house of the Estate, in which we lived for nine or ten months.' Published 1807. Classified among Poems dedicated to Independence and Liberty (No. XII).

1–4. The sea and the mountains are the most formidable barrier to invading tyrants, and islands and hilly countries are therefore the strongholds of liberty.

5. **There came a Tyrant**] In 1798 Switzerland had been invaded by French troops, under the pretext of a war of liberation: the old federal system of government had been overthrown, and the Helvetic republic had been established under French protection and upon the French model. The contest be-

tween the federalist and democratic parties and the unsettled state of the constitution of the republic made the new state of things unworkable, and Napoleon, then first consul, played upon the rival factions to secure the subjection of Switzerland to France. In 1802, after the withdrawal of the French army of occupation, civil war arose, and the federalists, under Aloys Reding, the *landamman* or chief magistrate of the republic, obtained some temporary success. A second invasion under Ney put an end to the disturbance and ensured French supremacy; and, by the act of mediation (1803), which granted Switzerland the shadow of independence and a new federal constitution, Napoleon practically disarmed her and made her powerless to offer any effective opposition to his plans. Wordsworth in 1820 visited the memorial to Aloys Reding near the lake of Thun and wrote the stanzas which form No. XIII of his *Memorials of a Tour on the Continent*. The original invasion in 1798 had given occasion to Coleridge's *France: an ode*, one of the finest of his poems.

12. **Mountain floods**] The mountain streams of Switzerland had exercised their fascination upon Wordsworth during his tour with Robert Jones in 1790. See *Descriptive Sketches* (1793), 161, 162:

> where Via Mala's chasms confine
> The indignant waters of the infant Rhine.

In 1824 the remembrance of the Via Mala came to him at the Devil's bridge in Cardiganshire:

> Or come the incessant shocks
> From that young Stream, that smites the throbbing rocks
> Of Viamala? There I seem to stand,
> As in life's morn; permitted to behold,
> From the dread chasm, woods climbing above woods,
> In pomp that fades not; everlasting snows;
> And skies that ne'er relinquish their repose:
> Such power possess the family of floods
> Over the minds of Poets, young or old!

SONG AT THE FEAST OF BROUGHAM CASTLE

Composed at Coleorton, 1807, in circumstances similar to those described in the introductory note to the preceding poem. Published in the *Poems* of that year. Classified among Poems of the Imagination (No. xxv). The story on which it is founded attracted Wordsworth for reasons which are amply explained in the four final stanzas. After the death of John, thirteenth baron Clifford and ninth baron of Westmorland, the Clifford of Shakespeare, 3 *Hen. VI*, at Ferrybridge in 1461, his young son Henry, a child of some six years old, was hidden by his mother, to escape the vengeance of the house of York, among shepherds in Cumberland. Here and at Londesborough in Yorkshire he lived in seclusion until, at the accession of Henry VII, he was restored to his father's honours. He fought at Flodden in 1513 and died in 1523: his son was created earl of Cumberland in 1525. The 'shepherd lord' spent much of his later life at Barden tower near Bolton priory, where he is said to have studied astrology: this is commemorated by Wordsworth in *The White Doe of Rylstone*, I, 264–307.

Brougham castle, of which the ruins remain, stands two miles S.E. of Penrith on the right bank of the Eamont, the river which has its source in Ullswater, near its junction with the Lowther. It was probably founded by Robert Vipont (*de Veteriponte*) in the reign of Henry II and came into the possession of the Cliffords by the marriage of his grand-daughter Isabel to Roger Clifford in the second quarter of the thirteenth century.

The *Song at the Feast of Brougham Castle* is Wordsworth's masterpiece in a type of poetry, founded on romantic legend, which he seldom attempted. The exaltation and enthusiasm of the song itself have a dramatic character of their own, which is emphasised by the contrast of the concluding stanzas, written in the reflective spirit habitual to Wordsworth.

27. The line is adapted from Sir John Beaumont's *Bosworth Field*, 1629, l. 100, where an angel says to Henry VII, 'the Avenger,'

' The Earth assists thee with the cry of blood.' Sir John Beaumont of Gracedieu, Leicestershire (1582-1628), was the brother of Francis Beaumont the dramatist and the ancestor of Sir George Howland Beaumont, in whose grounds at Coleorton this poem was composed. Cf. Wordsworth's inscription on a stone near a tree at Coleorton, ll. 17, 18:

> The haunt of him who sang how spear and shield
> In civil conflict met on Bosworth-field.

Bosworth is some eight or nine miles south of Coleorton.

34. **strong-abodes**] The peles or fortified houses common in the north of England, consisting of a tower or house round a courtyard, originally with an outer walled or palisaded enclosure.

36. **Skipton**] The castle of Skipton-in-Craven, which passed into the hands of the Cliffords, early in the fourteenth century. It was much added to by the Shepherd lord's son, the first earl of Cumberland, whose tomb is in Skipton church. The portion which he built is still standing and is one of the best remaining examples of a house of the reign of Henry VIII.

40. **Pendragon**] The ruins of this small castle stand close to the hamlet of Castlethwaite, four miles south of Kirkby Stephen, Westmorland, in the upper valley of the Eden.

44. **Brough**] Brough-under-Stainmore lies at the western foot of the fells which separate the valley of the Eden from that of the Tees. The castle, of which the ruins remain, has a history similar to that of Brougham. It stands at the meeting of the Augill and Swindale becks, a mile and a half above the confluence of the Swindale and Eden.

46. **she**] Appleby castle, standing on a hill at the south end of the town, round which the Eden curves in a semi-circle. This castle, like Brougham and Brough, came to the Cliffords from the Viponts.

56. This is not strictly accurate. The Shepherd lord was born about 1455, six years before his father's death.

73. **Carrock's side**] Carrock fell is a hill on the north-western border of the Lake country between Keswick and Carlisle.

It rises above Mosedale (l. 89), down which flows the Caldew, a tributary of the Eden.

90. **Blencathara**] Otherwise called Saddleback, a mountain south of Carrock fell, between it and Keswick. The Glenderamackin (l. 92) rises in Saddleback and, flowing past Threlkeld, enters Derwentwater at Keswick.

95. **Sir Lancelot Threlkeld**] This knight, who became the step-father of the 'Shepherd lord,' is said to have boasted 'that he possessed three noble houses—one for pleasure, Crosby in Westmorland, where he had a park well stocked with deer; one for profit and warmth, Yanwath, near Penrith; and one, Threlkeld, well stocked with tenants to go with him to the wars' (Murray's *Handbook to the English Lakes*, p. 80). Threlkeld hall and the tale of the Shepherd lord are referred to in *The Waggoner*, IV, 42 sqq.

122, 123. Bowscale tarn, in which a small stream tributary to the Caldew takes its rise, is at the foot of Bowscale fell, one of the northern outlying summits of the Saddleback range. Wordsworth notes: 'It is imagined by the people of the country that there are two immortal Fish, inhabitants of this Tarn, which lies in the mountains not far from Threlkeld.'

134. **Among the heavens**] 'There is a tradition current in the village of Threlkeld and its neighbourhood, his principal retreat, that in the course of his shepherd-life he had acquired great astronomical knowledge' (Wordsworth). See also introductory note with reference to his astrological studies.

137. **words of might**] Incantations. Cf. Scott, *The Lay of the Last Minstrel*, II, st. xiii:

> The words that cleft Eildon hills in three,
> And bridled the Tweed with a curb of stone.

140–64. These lines are cited by Coleridge (*Biog. Literaria*, ed. Ashe, pp. 200, 201) among examples of Wordsworth's use of a diction unmistakably his own. The bard's impassioned prophecy of war heightens the effect of the elegiac stanzas at the end of the poem, in which Wordsworth embodies a contrast congenial to the true lover and disciple of Nature.

161. Cf. *Excursion*, II, 62–4:

> Nor was he loth to enter ragged huts,
> Huts where his charity was blest: his voice
> Heard as the voice of an experienced friend.

The stanza, ll. 161-4, is an epitome of Wordsworth's own experience of the teaching of a simple life lived in communion with Nature. It is also a cardinal example of his power of communicating dignity to phrases of the simplest kind, to which are added a special beauty and glory which are the outcome of imagination touched by deep emotion.

GEORGE AND SARAH GREEN

Composed 1808. The incident upon which these lines were founded, the death of two peasants, whose home was in Easedale, near Grasmere, while returning across the fells from Great Langdale, took place during a heavy snow-storm in the winter of 1807-8. It is related with copious detail by De Quincey in his essay, *Early Memorials of Grasmere*, where the funeral of the couple in Grasmere churchyard is described and Wordsworth's verses are quoted. Pity for their fate was enhanced by admiration for the courage of their eldest daughter, a child of nine, who, snowed up with her brothers and sisters in their remote cottage, without knowledge of her parents' condition or means of communication with the outer world, met the responsibility with a tact and wisdom far beyond her years. Wordsworth's memorial of this episode is, like his earlier narratives, simplicity itself; but the verses, especially the last five stanzas, have a placid dignity and pathos which are typical of his power of identifying his style with his subject, and removing the natural barrier between thought and its expression in words.

11, 12. George Green fell over a precipice near the stream of White Ghyll, on the Langdale side of the fells. His wife's body was found at the summit. It was said afterwards that her cries were heard at Langdalehead through the snow-storm.

17–20. The day of the funeral 'happened to be in the most perfect contrast to the sort of weather which prevailed at the time of their misfortune: some snow still remained here and there upon the ground; but the azure of the sky was unstained by a cloud; and a golden sunlight seemed to sleep, so balmy and tranquil was the season, upon the very hills where the pair had wandered—then a howling wilderness, but now a green pastoral lawn, in its lower ranges, and a glittering expanse of virgin snow, in its higher.' (De Quincey.)

YARROW VISITED

September, 1814

No. IV of *Memorials of a Tour in Scotland*, 1814, published in 1815. See *Yarrow Unvisited* and notes, pp. 131–3 above. Wordsworth visited Yarrow in company with James Hogg, the 'Ettrick shepherd,' and Dr Robert Anderson, the editor of one of the standard collections of British Poets, walking from Traquair in the Tweed valley between Peebles and Galashiels. 'I seldom read or think of this poem,' wrote Wordsworth, 'without regretting that my dear Sister was not of the party, as she would have had so much delight in recalling the time when, travelling together in Scotland, we declined going in search of this celebrated stream, not altogether, I will frankly confess, for the reasons assigned in the poem on the occasion.'

5. **some Minstrel's harp**] An allusion to the title of *The Lay of the Last Minstrel.*

25. **the famous Flower**] The allusions in this and the next stanza are to the beautiful and tragic ballad by Hamilton of Bangour (see introd. note to *Yarrow Unvisited*, p. 131 above). But the 'Flower of Yarrow' was not the slain lover of the ballad,

the comliest swain
That eir pu'd birks on the Braes of Yarrow,

but a lady, celebrated in Scottish song, Mary Scott, daughter of

Philip Scott of Dryhope. She was married in 1567 to Walter Scott of Harden, from whom Sir Walter was descended in the sixth generation. See *The Lay of the Last Minstrel*, canto IV, st. ix.

31. **The Water-wraith]** The water-spirit, whose apparition foretold misfortune. Cf. Scott's ballad of *Rosabelle*, II, 12 (*Lay of the Last Minstrel*, VI, xxiii):

> The fishers have heard the Water-Sprite,
> Whose screams forebode that death is nigh,

and the two lines following,

> Last night the gifted Seer did view
> A wet shroud swathed round ladye gay.

49. Wordsworth leaves the solitudes round St Mary's loch and descends the vale of Yarrow towards Selkirk.

55. **Newark's Towers]** The castle of Newark (i.e. the new-work, a common medieval term for a building superseding or added to an older one) was a stronghold of the Scotts, ancestors of the dukes of Buccleuch, on the right bank of the Yarrow above Selkirk. It was at Newark that the Last Minstrel sang his lay to Anne, duchess of Buccleuch, widow of the duke of Monmouth, first duke of Buccleuch: see *Introd.* to the poem, 27, 28:

> He pass'd where Newark's stately tower
> Looks out from Yarrow's birchen bower.

69. Cf. *Intimations of Immortality*, 40 (p. 45 above).

COMPOSED UPON AN EVENING OF EXTRAORDINARY SPLENDOUR AND BEAUTY

This ode, composed in 1818, was published for the first time with the poems of 1820. The mood of serene reflection in which it was written and its profound sense of the spiritual beauty of the scene which it describes give it a place among the most characteristic poems of Wordsworth's middle life;

while they consciously repeat and emphasise the sentiments of the ode *Intimations of Immórtality*, with a conviction strengthened by advancing years. For Wordsworth's tone of calm content in this poem cf. ll. 200-3 of the same ode, p. 51 above.

1. **effulgence**] The splendour of the lingering sunset.

9. **Time was**] In the early days of earth, before the fall of man. See Adam's speech to Eve, Milton, *P. L.* IV, 677 sqq.:

> Millions of spiritual creatures walk the earth
> Unseen, both when we wake, and when we sleep, etc.

watery cove] A mountain recess with a tarn or stream within it. Cf. the description of the valley in Helvellyn in which lies the Red tarn, *Fidelity*, 17: ' It was a cove, a huge recess.'

22. **harmony**] Cf. the description of the silent harmony in all natural forms, *Excursion*, selection III, 21 sqq., p. 96 above.

35. **Informs my spirit**] Is the substance or indwelling being of my spirit.

40. **British shepherds**] The phrase is contrasted with ' Heaven's pomp ' in the previous line. Wordsworth's pride in his country and belief in the peculiar virtues of its peasants appear in the epithet.

41, 42. He turns from the serenity of the untroubled mind, which naturally is in union with the celestial vision, to the mind whose sense of the divine is obscured by earthly trouble.

43. **Yon hazy ridges**] Wordsworth notes: ' The multiplication of mountain-ridges, described......as a kind of Jacob's Ladder, leading to Heaven, is produced either by watery vapours, or sunny haze.'

49. The sight of this visionary ladder to heaven tempts him to imagine himself one of the angels for whom it is made.

52. **practicable**] I.e. that seems as if it really could be climbed.

55. **some traveller**] Like Jacob, Gen. xxviii, 11, 12.

57. **Ye Genii!**] The celestial beings whom imagination sees as the guardian angels of the scene.

61. **Such hues**] Cf. the opening lines of *Intimations of Immortality* and the idea of 'the glory and the gleam' and 'the vision splendid' of childhood and youth which is the fundamental idea of the poem. This moment belongs to 'a season of calm weather' in which the visions of childhood are remembered and renewed, and

> Our Souls have sight of that immortal sea
> Which brought us hither.

69. **Dread Power!**] Cf. *Ode to Duty*, 16, p. 40 above.

79. **the visionary splendour fades**] Just as, in *Intimations of Immortality*, 75, 76, the 'vision splendid' fades 'into the light of common day.' The vision is but transitory, and man returns to reality from the high imaginations which it calls forth.

WRITTEN UPON A BLANK LEAF IN 'THE COMPLETE ANGLER'

Dated by Wordsworth and published 1819. Classified among Misc. sonnets (I, xvi). Cf. the sonnet on *Walton's Book of Lives*, p. 75 above. Izaak Walton (1593-1683) published *The Compleat Angler* in 1653: a second part, by Charles Cotton, was added to it in 1676.

9. **sedgy Lee**] The Lea, which rises on the borders of Hertfordshire and Bedfordshire, and, after passing Hertford and Ware, divides Hertfordshire and Middlesex from Essex and falls into the Thames near Blackwall. The scene of the dialogues of the first part of *The Compleat Angler* is laid on the banks of the Lea.

10. **Shawford brook**] Mentioned by Walton in a lyric in *The Compleat Angler*, I, 5:

> Or—with my *Bryan*, and a book—
> Loiter long-days near *Shawford-brook*.

One of Walton's commentators says: 'Shawford-brook is the name of that part of the river Sow that runs through the land which Walton bequeathed to the corporation of Stafford, to find coals for the poor.'

TO THE REV. DR WORDSWORTH

These stanzas, composed at Christmas, 1819, form the dedication to *The River Duddon* sonnets (see note on p. 156 below). They are addressed to the poet's younger brother Christopher, born 1774, who was at this time rector of Lambeth, and the year after became master of Trinity college, Cambridge (1820-41). He died in 1846. His son Christopher (1807-85), head-master of Harrow 1836, and bishop of Lincoln 1868-85, was the object of one of Wordsworth's sonnets (Misc. sonnets, III, xl), written in 1843. Wordsworth, contrasting his own lot with his brother's choice of ecclesiastical preferment, enlarges upon the benefits of his peaceful life among his native hills and upon his favourite theme of the ennobling simplicity of pastoral manners.

5. **a rich and dazzling sheen**] See *Excursion*, selection VI, 5–13, p. 100 above, for a description of the transforming power of the moon upon foliage.

7–10. The stillness of a frosty night, interrupted by the music of the waits, could not be more beautifully described. For ll. 7, 8 cf. Coleridge, *Frost at midnight*, I, 2:

> The Frost performs its secret ministry,
> Unhelped by any wind.

29. **these rustic Powers**] The influences of the natural features of rural life. The light on the faces of those who listen to the Christmas strain is a revival of the happiness known in days when 'meadow, grove, and stream' were 'apparelled in celestial light' to the youthful imagination.

40. **at an earlier call**] I.e. earlier in the evening, while all are still seated round the fire.

42. **self-complacent innocence**] He refers to the hush of children, as they listen to the music outside. Their innocence is self-complacent in the best sense: they are contented with thoughts and occupations which they have not yet learned to measure with those of others, and consequently cannot as yet feel dissatisfaction with themselves.

49–60. It is not merely for the sake of its natural beauty that Wordsworth loves his native soil. Love of Man combines with love of Nature. The old-fashioned customs of the country-side are also dear to him: their preservation is a sure guarantee of simplicity and generosity of character, and the mountains, which prevent too much contact with the busy outside world, are the guardians which ensure the survival of such character and customs together. The bond between man and Nature which these lines emphasise is illustrated by the narrative of *Michael*, Wordsworth's most successful tribute to the unity of the unspoiled pastoral character with its natural surroundings.

50. **ambient**] Flowing round the field.

51. **Cytherea's zone**] The magic girdle of Aphrodite, which gave her the power of inspiring love. Aphrodite is called Cytherea from the island of Cythera in the Aegean, one of the chief seats of her worship. It was near this place that, according to one legend, she rose from the sea.

52. **the Thunderer**] Zeus.

55. **ancient Manners!**] The view of the power of the simple pastoral life to breed fortitude of character and give nobility to a nation appears in Vergil, *Georgics*, II, 458 sqq., where rustic simplicity and manners like those of the golden age are praised as the foundation of the glories of Rome. See also Horace, *Carmina*, III, iii, 33–44, where the 'rusticorum mascula militum proles,' the peasant army of the Roman republic, trained by hard work in the fields, is contrasted with its degenerate successors.

67–9. Those who fail, amid days of strenuous occupation, to find even short periods of leisure, may make for themselves leisure even in the midst of their business, and so gain moments of rest in which the memory recalls the past. Wordsworth contrasts the enforced want of bodily leisure with the mental leisure which depends upon an act of the will.

74. **frequent**] Incessantly. The original sense of the Latin *frequens* is 'constantly repeated': thus the adjective is applied

to crowds assembled in large numbers, i.e. consisting of repetitions of the human form. Wordsworth had this application in his mind: the din of London is the result of crowded movement of men and traffic.

satiate] Cf. *Excursion*, selection VIII, 48, p. 104 above.

77. **overwhelm nor cloy**] The din of the city at once overwhelms with its uproar and satiates with its monotony.

SONNETS

FROM THE RIVER DUDDON

The River Duddon: a series of sonnets, written at intervals during a period of many years, was published in May, 1820, with the dedicatory poem in thirteen stanzas to Wordsworth's brother Christopher, printed on pp. 67–70 above. The Duddon rises near the Wrynose pass, above the head of Little Langdale, and near the Three-shire stone, which marks the meeting of Cumberland, Westmorland and Lancashire. Flowing S.S.W., it forms the boundary between Cumberland and Lancashire for about 20 miles, and enters the Irish sea through the estuary of the Duddon sands, which divides the southern extremity of Cumberland from Furness. The sonnets are characteristic of Wordsworth's quiet delight in rural beauty. Taking suggestions from casual objects seen in the course of the river's progress, he spiritualises them and sacrifices mere description to the inner meaning which they hold for the imagination. The four selected here are typical of the series. Sonnets I–III are concerned with the source of the stream in the bare fells:

> to chant thy birth, thou hast
> No meaner Poet than the whistling Blast,
> And Desolation is thy Patron-saint!

In sonnets IV–VIII it is traced through its upper valley, amid the first signs of human habitation, until in sonnet IX

> The struggling Rill insensibly is grown
> Into a Brook of loud and stately march.

Sonnets IX–XXXI wander discursively through the lower part of the valley and the villages and hamlets of Seathwaite, Dunnerdale and Ulpha. In sonnets XXXII and XXXIII the river enters the sea,

> Majestic Duddon, over smooth flat sands
> Gliding in silence with unfettered sweep,

and the poet concludes with the aspiration

> And may thy Poet, cloud-born Stream, be free—
> The sweets of earth contentedly resigned,
> And each tumultuous working left behind
> At seemly distance—to advance like Thee;
> Prepared, in peace of heart, in calm of mind
> And soul, to mingle with Eternity!

Sonnet XXXIV is an after-thought, summing up the parallel between the perennial course of the stream and the never-dying function of humanity to which each mortal life contributes.

V

6. **green alders**] Cf. the 'alder shades' of Derwent, *Prelude*, I, 272. See note on *Intimations of Immortality*, 192, 193 (p. 144 above).

13, 14. Lonely Nature is a source of pure pleasure to the children in their solitary cottage-home: their life and its surroundings are a perpetual summer, free from care.

XXI

2. **when here I roved**] All this neighbourhood was familiar to Wordsworth during his school-days at Hawkshead, recorded in *Prelude*, I, 11.

9. **stall**] Seat, a word most commonly used in connexion with the stalls in the quire of a church.

12. **golden locks of birch**] Wordsworth's thought attaches itself to the autumnal foliage of the trees in the valley, moved gently by the breeze, the outward symbol of the 'whisper from the heart' that awakens his memory in the autumn of his life.

XXVI

1. In sonnet xxv Wordsworth has lamented the absence of Dorothy

> The One for whom my heart shall ever beat
> With tenderest love

from the resting-place which he has found in the valley.

> With sweets that she partakes not some distaste
> Mingles, and lurking consciousness of wrong;
> Languish the flowers; the waters seem to waste
> Their vocal charm; their sparklings cease to please.

The memory, however, of what streams have meant to his youth recalls him to contented meditation and gratitude.

4. **with flying inquest**] Cf. *Tintern Abbey*, 66–72, p. 7 above.

5. **The sullen reservoirs**] The mountain-tarns. Cf. note on 'watery cove,' p. 152 above, l. 9.

XXXIV

1. **thee**] The river, which he has watched

> in radiant progress toward the Deep
> Where mightiest rivers into powerless sleep
> Sink, and forget their nature,

and has likened, at its meeting with the sea, to the soul bound on its progress from life to eternity (see introd. note). Looking back, he sees the stream still ceaselessly flowing from its inexhaustible source, and is reminded that the individual human soul is merely a part of the constantly flowing river of humanity.

6. **The Form**] The actual being which exists permanently beneath the superficial accidents which give it changing aspects. To this form is attached a function which is equally permanent. Cf. Shelley, *Adonais*, 460:

> The One remains, the many change and pass.

Thus (ll. 8–14) the individual mortal is but a passing shape taken by the form of humanity, and his efforts are contributions to the eternal function belonging to that form. His real greatness is measured by the permanent influence of such contributions upon humanity.

HYMN FOR THE BOATMEN

No. IX of *Memorials of a Tour on the Continent*, 1820, in the original edition, 1822: later no. X. The Wordsworths landed at Calais, 11 July, 1820, and proceeded by way of Bruges, Ghent, Brussels, Namur, Liège and Aix-la-Chapelle to Cologne. They then followed the banks of the Rhine upwards, reached Mainz on 25 July, and were at Frankfurt-am-Main the next day. They were at Heidelberg on the 27th, and left Heidelberg for Carlsruhe on the 28th. The river at Heidelberg is the Neckar, which joins the Rhine at Mannheim, about 15 miles lower down. Dorothy Wordsworth, who accompanied her brother and his wife, wrote a journal of the tour. This simple and beautiful lyric illustrates the religious aspect of Wordsworth's later poetry, which is conspicuous also in his *Ecclesiastical Sonnets* and in *The Labourer's Noonday Hymn*, 'Up to the throne of God is borne,' a dignified composition intended to supply a companion piece to bishop Ken's morning and evening hymns.

8. **Rood**] The old English word for a cross, specially applied to the cross on which Christ suffered.

13. **yon ancient Tower**] The castle of the electors palatine, the elder branch of the Bavarian house of Wittelsbach and rulers of the Rhenish palatinate. Heidelberg is now in the grand duchy of Baden. The castle, a splendid ruin of red sandstone standing high on the wooded left bank of the river, was abandoned in 1764. The octagonal tower at the north-east corner is a distinguishing feature of the view from the river.

24. **Miserere Domine**] Have mercy, O Lord.

THE SOURCE OF THE DANUBE

No. x (afterwards No. xi) of *Memorials of a Tour on the Continent.* Wordsworth's visit to the source of the Danube at Donaueschingen in the grand duchy of Baden is not recorded in Dorothy Wordsworth's journal, the dates of which at this point are not very trustworthy. The travellers appear, however, to have passed through Donaueschingen on 31 July or 1 August. They reached Zurich on 3 August, having visited Schaffhausen and the falls of the Rhine in the interval.

1. **his great Compeers**] E.g. the Rhine and the Rhone, springing in torrents from the glaciers of the Alps.

4. In 1820, the lower course of the Danube lay for the most part within the Ottoman empire.

8. **that gloomy sea**] The *Pontus Euxinus* or Black sea.

9. **the Orphean lyre**] Orpheus, according to one legend, went with the Argonauts on their voyage, and overcame many of their difficulties with the music of his lyre, which charmed and fixed in their places the Symplegades, the moving rocks fabled to defend the entrance from the Bosporus to the Euxine.

11, 12. The Argo was said to have been made into a constellation by the goddess Pallas.

COMPOSED IN ONE OF THE CATHOLIC CANTONS

Originally part of the poem on *The Church of San Salvador seen from the Lake of Lugano,* which is variously numbered xxiii and xxiv in later editions of *Memorials of a Tour on the Continent.* These stanzas were separated from the rest in *Poetical Works,* 1827, and in modern editions are numbered xiv or xv in the same series of poems. In their spirit of charity and sympathy with a form of religion to which their author did not subscribe they recall the wise reflections of Sir Thomas Browne, *Religio Medici,* i, § 3, where he says of Romanists: 'We have reformed from them, not against them; for omitting those improperations and terms of scurrility betwixt us, which only difference our affections, and not our cause, there is between us one common name and appellation, one faith and necessary body of principles common to us both; and therefore I am not scrupulous to converse and live with them, to enter their churches in defect of ours, and either pray with them, or for them.' The Wordsworths were at Lugano on 27 and 28 Aug. 1820. The furthest point of their tour was Milan (2 and 3 Sept.), from which they returned into Switzerland by way of the Simplon pass. They travelled into France by way of Chamouni and the lake of Geneva, and returned to England at the beginning of November.

9. **the firm, unmoving cross]** Cf. *Prelude*, VIII, 273-5: see note on *Michael* (I), 20 (pp. 116, 117 above). See also *Prelude*, VI, 480-8, where Wordsworth describes how, near the Grande Chartreuse, he and his friend saw

> In different quarters of the bending sky,
> The cross of Jesus stand erect, as if
> Hands of angelic powers had fixed it there.

WALTON'S BOOK OF LIVES

From *Ecclesiastical Sonnets*, part III, v. This series of 132 sonnets, divided into three parts, was published in 1822, most of the collection having been composed in the previous year. For Walton see note on the sonnet *Written upon a blank leaf in 'The Complete Angler,'* p. 153 above. The five biographies constituting his *Lives* were published separately at intervals between 1640 and 1678. Wordsworth admirably characterises the simplicity and devoutness of spirit of these tributes to piety and learning.

6. The statesman is Sir Henry Wotton (1568-1639). 'Priest' applies equally to the subjects of the four remaining lives, John Donne, dean of St Paul's (1573-1631), Richard Hooker (d. 1600), George Herbert (1593–1633), and Robert Sanderson, bishop of

Lincoln (1587–1663). The 'humble Citizen' is Walton himself, who, for some twenty years before the outbreak of the civil war, was a draper in Fleet street: the *Lives* are the unconscious revelation of his own character.

10. **glow-worms**] In Wordsworth's earliest published poem, *An Evening Walk*, occur lines (267, 268) describing the glow-worm's light:

> While others, not unseen, are free to shed
> Green unmolested light upon their mossy bed.

In their original form, these lines ran:

> while on the ground
> Small circles of green radiance gleam around.

The phrase 'green radiance' was quoted by Coleridge, *Lines written at Shurton Bars*, 4–6:

> I mark the glow-worm, as I pass,
> Move with 'green radiance' through the grass,
> An emerald of light.

Allusions to the glow-worm are frequent in Wordsworth. For the present passage, cf. *The Pilgrim's Dream, or the Star and the Glow-worm*, written in 1818, 60–4:

> And all the happy Souls that rode
> Transfigured through that fresh abode,
> Had heretofore, in humble trust,
> Shone meekly 'mid their native dust,
> The Glow-worms of the earth.

11. **lonely tapers**] Cf. Shakespeare, *Merchant of Venice*, v, i, 90, 91:

> How far that little candle throws his beams!
> So shines a good deed in a naughty world.

SCORN NOT THE SONNET

Published in 1827. Classified among Miscellaneous sonnets (II, i). Wordsworth says that it was 'composed almost extempore, in a short walk on the western side of Rydal Lake.' Cf. the kindred sonnet 'Nuns fret not at their convent's narrow room.'

3. **Shakespeare**] Wordsworth adopted the much controverted view that Shakespeare's sonnets are autobiographical. Browning, in the poem called *House*, disputed the inference that Shakespeare wore his heart on his sleeve for all the world to see:

> '*With this key*
> *Shakespeare unlocked his heart,*' once more!
> Did Shakespeare? If so, the less Shakespeare he!

4. **Petrarch's wound**] Francesco Petrarca (1304–74), whose Italian poems, consisting of sonnets interspersed with *canzoni* or odes, celebrated his devotion to Laura. Of Laura little is known, save that her name was Laure de Noves and that she was the wife of Hugues de Sade, a nobleman whose estates lay near Avignon.

5. **Tasso**] Torquato Tasso (1544–95), more celebrated for his epic, *La Gerusalemme Liberata*, which gave him his place, with Dante, Petrarch and Ariosto, among the four great poets of Italy.

6. **Camoëns**] Luis de Camoes (1524–79), the Portuguese epic poet, author of *The Lusiad* (*Os Lusiadas*). He fell into disgrace at court on account of a love-affair, commemorated in his sonnets, and was exiled to his home at Santarem. After taking part in the expedition to Ceuta in Africa, he returned to Lisbon, but soon found it desirable to leave Portugal again. After a chequered career of war and travel in the East Indies, he came under the displeasure of the viceroy at Goa and was banished to Macao, where he completed his epic. The last ten years of his life were spent in comparative obscurity and neglect in Portugal.

8. **Dante**] The sonnets of Dante Alighieri (1265–1321) are included in his *Canzoniere* or book of miscellaneous poems and in *La Vita Nuova*, the mystical record of his devotion to Beatrice de' Portinari. They have been translated into English verse by D. G. Rossetti in his volume, *The Early Italian Poets*, and its revised form, *Dante and his Circle*. Although they naturally have not the sustained grandeur of his great visionary epic, *La Divina Commedia*, and their language is more conventional, the contrast is less marked than is implied by Wordsworth, and gaiety is not their prevailing characteristic.

9. **a glow-worm lamp**] See note on *Walton's Book of Lives*, l. 10, p. 162 above.

10. **Spenser**] Spenser's *Amoretti*, a series of sonnets published in 1595, were written in honour of his wife, Elizabeth Boyle, and actually belong to the period before the final misfortunes of his life fell upon him. They were contemporary with the composition of the later books of *The Faerie Queene*.

12. **Milton**] For the influence of his sonnets upon Wordsworth, see introd. note to *London*, 1802, p. 124 above. In a note to 'Nuns fret not at their convent's narrow room' Wordsworth says that he was impelled to sonnet-writing one afternoon in 1801, after Dorothy had read Milton's sonnets to him. He immediately produced three sonnets, 'the first I ever wrote except an irregular one at school.' Of these, the one beginning 'I grieved for Buonaparte' was printed in *The Morning Post*, 6 Dec. 1802. Dorothy Wordsworth (*Journals*, I, 123) gives the actual date of these first sonnets as 21 May, 1802, which shews that Wordsworth was a year wrong in the date attributed to them.

GLAD SIGHT WHEREVER NEW WITH OLD

This little lyric, belonging to Wordsworth's latest period of work, about 1845, but recalling the fresh enthusiasm of such poems as the lines on the rainbow (p. 23 above), was published in 1845. Classified among Poems of the Fancy (No. xx).

THE UNREMITTING VOICE OF NIGHTLY STREAMS

Composed in 1846; published in the collected ed. of 1849–50 (Poems of Sentiment and Reflection, No. xxxii). The perpetual presence of the voice of waters among the hills was one of the manifestations of Nature to which Wordsworth most frequently recurred. See, e.g., *Prelude,* selection v, 20, 21, and *Excursion,* selection vii, 18–20, pp. 85, 101 above.

1. **nightly**] At night-time. See note on *Excursion,* selection v, ii, p. 186 below.

3. **the worm**] See note on *Walton's Book of Lives,* 10, p. 162 above.

7–9. Man's intelligence is insufficient to comprehend the full purpose of the gifts of Nature, or to accuse her of excess and waste in some things and defect in others. Heaven's estimate of its gifts is different from human notions of extravagance and niggardliness. Cf. *Eccl. Sonnets,* iii, xliii (*Inside of King's college chapel, Cambridge,* 6, 7):

> Give all thou canst; high Heaven rejects the lore
> Of nicely-calculated less or more.

10. **a healing influence**] Such as Matthew Arnold discovered in the 'unpretending harmony' of Wordsworth's own poetry: see *Memorial Verses, April,* 1850, 62, 63:

> But where will Europe's latter hour
> Again find Wordsworth's healing power?

14. **murmuring brooks**] Cf. the thanks offered by the votary to the genius of the stream Cephisus in *Excursion,* iv, 745 sqq., where the stream that takes his offering awakens the thought 'of Life continuous, Being unimpaired.' See also the passage quoted in the note on *Intimations of Immortality,* 192, 193, p. 144 above.

17. **water-breaks**] Places where the full flow of a stream is interrupted by stones or rocks, and the water ripples through in narrow channels and rapids.

SELECTIONS FROM THE PRELUDE

The Prelude; or, Growth of a Poet's Mind; an autobiographical poem was intended to be, as its title indicates, a preparatory poem to the main work of his life, *The Recluse*, of which only the second part, *The Excursion*, was finished. It was begun in Germany in 1799, and the first two books were written chiefly then and at Grasmere in 1800. The remaining twelve books were composed in 1804 and 1805, earlier fragments being occasionally worked into their fabric. The whole poem was recited by Wordsworth to Coleridge, to whom it was dedicated, at Coleorton in Jan. 1807; but it was not published until 1850, after Wordsworth's death and long after the publication of *The Excursion* (1814). In his preface to *The Excursion* he mentioned *The Prelude*, likening its relation to *The Excursion* as that which 'the Ante-chapel has to the body of a Gothic church,' and intimating that his shorter poems, when properly arranged, would 'be found by the attentive reader to have such connection with the main work as may give them claim to be likened to the little cells, oratories, and sepulchral recesses, ordinarily included in those edifices.' *The Prelude* and *The Excursion* are, in fact, the summing-up of Wordsworth's theory of life and poetry, and, by reference to them, the reader learns to co-ordinate the rest of his work; and *The Prelude* in particular, amid its autobiographical detail and elaborate analysis of ideas, is full of passages which bear eloquent witness to the beauty of Wordsworth's thought and the calm splendour of his imagination in his highest activity.

I. THE DISCIPLINE OF NATURE

From book I (*Childhood and School-time*), 340–475. This famous passage, illustrating the influence of Nature upon Wordsworth's boyhood at Hawkshead, is one of the chief keys to the understanding of his poetry. In ll. 1-17 he analyses the various ministries which Nature employs to arouse and fortify the human spirit, laying special stress upon the impressions of love and fear which are received from her visitations. An instance of the 'severer interventions' which instil awe into her votary is given in ll. 18–61. The immortal Spirit which informs Nature is apostrophised in ll. 62–75: its influence upon the soul, associating its passions 'with high objects, with enduring things,' purifies and ennobles it. Instances of solitary intercourse with Nature and its effect follow in ll. 76–124, and in ll. 125–36 the subject of the whole passage is reviewed and summed up.

1, 2. Our mortal bodies are composed of dust, but our spirits are made up of immortal elements, the discord between which is resolved into harmony by a mysterious and secret power, the indwelling Spirit which animates and reconciles all the different forms of Nature. See note on *Tintern Abbey*, 94–102, p. 111 above.

14. **with soft alarm**] These gentler visitations, in which Nature fills the mind with pleasurable surprise, are referred to in *Prelude*, I, 586, as 'gleams like the flashing of a shield.'

17. **More palpable**] I.e. conveying a more distinct and sensible impression.

22. **the shore**] Of Esthwaite water, the lake at the north end of which Hawkshead is situated.

34. **an elfin pinnace**] A fairy, i.e. tiny, fragile boat.

39. **a huge peak**] Wetherlam, 2520 feet high, about 5 miles N.W. of Hawkshead.

40. **with voluntary power instinct**] Imbued with a will of its own.

46. **Strode after me**] I.e. to punish him for his 'act of stealth' (l. 22).

62–5. See note on *Tintern Abbey*, 94–102, p. 111 above.

89-124. These lines were published, with some slight variations in phrase and considerable differences in punctuation, as a separate poem by Coleridge in *The Friend* for 28 Dec. 1809, and appeared in the collected edition of Wordsworth's poems in 1815. They were subsequently classified among Poems referring to the period of Childhood (No. XVI) under the title, *Influence of Natural Objects in calling forth and strengthening the imagination in boyhood and early youth.*

96. **Confederate, imitative**] The first adjective is in apposition to 'we', the subject of the sentence; while the second refers to 'games.'

100–5. For the influence of mountain echoes on Wordsworth see l. 24 above, and cf. note on *To Joanna*, 56–66, pp. 121, 122 above.

111. **reflex**] Reflection.

112. This line, in the fragment as published separately, ran 'Image that, flying still before me, gleamed.' In l. 88 'blazed through twilight gloom' stood in the separate version as 'through the twilight blazed,' and 'a dreamless sleep' in l. 124 stood as 'a summer sea.' The alterations in the final form of the poem are all for the better.

121. **diurnal**] Daily. Cf. *A slumber did my spirit seal*, 7: 'Rolled round in earth's diurnal course'; and *Excursion*, III, 613:

> Her annual, her diurnal, round alike
> Maintained with faithful care.

123. **Feebler and feebler**] As he stands still, the apparent movement of the banks on each side of him gradually ceases and comes to a stop.

125. **Ye Presences of Nature**] I.e. the various forms under which the one Presence manifests itself.

128. **A vulgar hope**] A merely ordinary hope. Wordsworth recognises that the incessant promptings with which natural objects filled his mind had a special purpose, destining him for a career in which he was to be Nature's chosen servant and poet.

II. NATURE THE SOURCE OF HOPE AND COURAGE

From book II (*School-time*), 419–51.

1. **If this be error**] In the lines preceding this passage Wordsworth had described his impression of 'the sentiment of Being' in all created things and the transport which it awakens

in his heart. He realises that this sense of the community of life, proceeding from the uncreated source of Being, is closely akin to the doctrine of pantheism, according to which the revelation of God consists in His immanence in creation. The 'pious mind' is more ready to accept a faith which lays stress upon a personal Creator than a faith which seems to merge His personality in His creations.

6. **ye mountains, and ye lakes**] Cf. Coleridge's address (*Fears in Solitude*, 182 sqq.) to his 'Mother Isle,' where he refers to

thy lakes and mountain-hills,
Thy clouds, thy quiet dales, thy rocks and seas,

as the source of his intellectual life and of

Whatever makes this mortal spirit feel
The joy and greatness of its future being.

See also *Frost at Midnight*, 54 sqq., where he prophesies the future happiness which his child will win from solitary communion with Nature.

7. **sounding cataracts**] Cf. *Tintern Abbey*, 76. 77, p. 8 above.

14. **these times of fear**] The first two books of *The Prelude* were written in 1799 and 1800, when Wordsworth's early political enthusiasm had been disappointed. It was now, when his former confidence failed him, that he found his support and consolation in the lessons of Nature, whose unchangeableness revived his hope for humanity and himself. The conviction

that Nature never did betray
The heart that loved her

(*Tintern Abbey*, 122, 123) is expressed here with fuller emphasis.

25. **A more than Roman confidence**] He is thinking of the patriotism of the heroes of the Roman republic, whose faith in the state and liberty upheld them through disaster. His own confidence, rooted in the eternity of Nature, is even surer and stronger.

III. ST JOHN'S COLLEGE, CAMBRIDGE

From book III (*Residence at Cambridge*), 46–63.

1. **St John**] The college of St John the Evangelist, founded in 1511 by the executors of Margaret, countess of Richmond and Derby, mother of Henry VII. The three courts by which the college had been gradually enlarged in the sixteenth and seventeenth centuries were augmented between 1825 and 1831 by the addition of a fourth court across the river, approached by the covered bridge known as the Bridge of Sighs.

2. **in the first**] Wordsworth's rooms were on the first floor at the south-west corner of the first court. They are now incorporated in the kitchen offices, which have been enlarged since his time.

5. **tuneable**] Tuneful. Cf. Milton, *P. L.* v, 151.

8. **Trinity's loquacious clock**] The great court of Trinity is separated only by a narrow lane from the buildings of St John's in which Wordsworth lived. The chapel forms the eastern part of the range of buildings next this lane, and at its west end is King Edward's gateway, in the tower above which is the clock referred to.

15. **the statue**] Roubiliac's statue of Sir Isaac Newton (fellow of Trinity 1667–1727, Lucasian professor of mathematics 1669–1702, and M.P. for the University) stands at the west end of the ante-chapel of Trinity. De Quincey, reading this passage carelessly, as others have done since his day, imagined that the statue was actually visible from Wordsworth's rooms 'through the great windows in the adjacent chapel of Trinity.' This, however, is not stated by Wordsworth.

IV. A SUMMER DAWN

From book IV (*Summer Vacation*), 319-38. This view of a summer dawn, to which Wordsworth looked back as marking an epoch in his life, was an incident in a period at which he was somewhat distracted from the service of Nature by trivial amusements. He was returning home after a night spent 'in dancing, gaiety, and mirth,' when Nature gave him this reminder of her presence and impressed upon him, as yet unconscious, the vocation to which he was ultimately destined. He describes, in the lines which follow this passage, the state of his mind at the time:

> A parti-coloured show of grave and gay,
> Solid and light, short-sighted and profound:
> Of inconsiderate habits and sedate,
> Consorting in one mansion unreproved.

10. **Grain-tinctured**] Coloured in grain, i.e. the inequalities of the surface of the mountains could be seen distinctly, forming lines and spaces of colour and shadow.

empyrean light] Light like that of the highest heaven, the sphere of fire, from the Greek ἔμπυρος (*émpyros*) = fiery. The word occurs frequently in Milton, e.g. *P. L.* II, 771: 'through all the Empyrean.' Cf. *ibid.* VII, 12–14:

> Up led by thee
> Into the heav'n of heav'ns I have presum'd
> An earthly guest, and drawn empyreal air.

Wordsworth's debt to Milton for the form and phraseology of his blank verse is noticeable in this passage, which should also be compared with *Prelude*, x, 514 sqq., the description of his walk across the sands of Morecambe bay in July, 1794.

14. **labourers**] Human beings are added to the scene. Wordsworth is speaking of the days before he had fully realised 'the still sad music of humanity,' and these figures, like the rest of the landscape, impressed themselves upon his eye primarily from the point of view of their picturesque value. In the light

of later knowledge, he recognises the full influence of these details upon his mind. He enlarges in *Prelude*, VIII, 340 sqq., upon the gradual growth of his appreciation of man from the time when man was entirely subordinate in his affections to Nature:

a passion, she,
A rapture often, and immediate love
Ever at hand; he, only a delight
Occasional, an accidental grace,
His hour being not yet come.

15. **dear Friend**] Coleridge.

16. **I made no vows**] He drank in the beauty of the scene without the conscious sense that the presence which filled it was acting upon him and forging a bond between itself and him. The meaning of the 'thankful blessedness' (l. 20) which he felt was not realised till later; but his remembrance of this feeling enabled him to point to this moment as an epoch in his spiritual life. Cf. the similar passage in *Excursion*, I, 197–218, especially ll. 214 sqq.:

No thanks he breathed, he proffered no request;
Rapt into still communion that transcends
The imperfect offices of prayer and praise,
His mind was a thanksgiving to the power
That made him; it was blessedness and love!

V. THE BOY OF WINDERMERE

From book V (*Books*), 364–97. These lines were written in Germany at the close of 1798 and were published in 1800. They subsequently formed No. I of Poems of the Imagination. Wordsworth writes: 'This practice of making an instrument of their own fingers is known to most boys, though some are more skilful at it than others. William Raincock of Rayrigg, a fine spirited lad, took the lead of all my schoolfellows in this art.'

2. **Winander**] Windermere. Rayrigg is on the east side of the lake, near Bowness.

16, 17. In their earlier form, these lines ran:

And, when there came a pause
Of silence such as baffled his best skill.

18. **hung**] Waited in suspense.

20, 21. **the voice Of mountain torrents**] Cf. *An Evening Walk*, 365–8:

The song of mountain-streams, unheard by day,
Now hardly heard, beguiles my homeward way,
Air listens, like the sleeping water, still,
To catch the spiritual music of the hill.

Dorothy Wordsworth (*Journals*, II, 211) says: 'All night, and all day, and for ever, the vale of Meiringen is sounding with torrents'; and of Glenfalloch, the 'hidden vale' at the head of Loch Lomond (12 Sept. 1803): 'We sate down, and heard, as if from the heart of the earth, the sound of torrents ascending out of the long hollow glen. To the eye all was motionless, a perfect stillness. The noise of waters did not appear to come this way or that, from any particular quarter: it was everywhere, almost, one might say, as if "exhaled" through the whole surface of the green earth.'

24. **uncertain**] The 'uncertain heaven' may be the reflection of the sky in the lake, forming a visionary picture which raises the doubt whether it is really a reflection. Cf. the sonnet *Composed by the side of Grasmere Lake*, 9–11, p. 42 above. It may, however, refer merely to the changes of the sky itself, as the stars rise and set (ll. 3–5).

VI. THE SIMPLON PASS

From book VI (*Cambridge and the Alps*), 621–40. These lines, describing the descent of the Simplon pass, were published separately, with slight variations, in 1845. Classified among Poems of the Imagination, No. VII. Wordsworth crossed the Simplon on his walking tour with Robert Jones in 1790: some features of this tour were the subject of one of his earliest poems, *Descriptive Sketches*, but it was described more connectedly and its influence upon his imagination traced in *The Prelude*. In Sept. 1820, he revisited the Simplon, crossing it in the opposite direction. In the interval between the two visits, the carriage-road over the pass had been constructed by order of Napoleon I. The pass, over 6000 feet at its highest point, crosses the Alps from Brieg in the Rhone valley to Domo d' Ossola in Piedmont.

2. **this gloomy strait**] The gorge of Gondo, 'one of the grandest and most gloomy in the Alps. It is bounded by slate-rocks, whose smooth vertical sides deny support to any vegetation. At the base of these cliffs and in the bed of the stream are heaped the ruins of the mountains; while loosened masses still hanging on the slope seem to threaten the passenger' (Murray, *Hand-book to Switzerland*). The mountain-torrent which flows through the gorge is called the Diveria.

6. **stationary blasts**] The noise of the waterfalls was like the blast of trumpet after trumpet, each continuing ceaselessly in its own allotted station. Cf. *Intimations of Immortality*, 25, p. 44 above.

12. **the sick sight**] The stream, as seen from the pass, raves in its bed with the restlessness of a sick man. 'Giddy prospect' (l. 13) is, on the other hand, the effect which this restlessness has directly upon the eye.

16–20. Each feature of the scene becomes a token of the indwelling presence which interfuses itself in all Nature and 'reconciles discordant elements' into harmony. Each is, as it were, one of the visible characters in which the revelation of this presence is written (l. 18), and is a symbol of the eternal unseen Being which thus manifests itself through concrete objects (ll. 19, 20).

VII. ASCENT OF SNOWDON

From book XIV (*Conclusion*), 11–62. The night-ascent of Snowdon from Beddgelert, described in this passage, was made by Wordsworth in the summer of 1791, during a walking tour taken in company with Robert Jones. Wordsworth uses this experience as a symbol of thoughts on which he proceeds to enlarge. The moon in the clear firmament, gazing down upon the sea of mist and the billow-like hill-tops, is

> the emblem of a mind
> That feeds upon infinity, that broods
> Over the dark abyss, intent to hear
> Its voices issuing forth to silent light
> In one continuous stream.

Such a mind idealises all sensible objects, associating them with ideas of 'transcendent power.' It shares also the influence, which Nature exercises over man, of leading others by its own secret force to hear, see and feel. In its converse with the infinite, it is detached from the enthralment of the world in which it lives; but it is quick to catch suggestions from its concrete surroundings and give them spiritual form. Such a mind is an emanation of the Deity, a Power in itself. Its consciousness of its orgin, its perpetual communion with Heaven, are the springs of its daily life, its cheerfulness and fortitude amid adversity,

> that peace
> Which passeth understanding, that repose
> In moral judgments which from this pure source
> Must come, or will by man be sought in vain.

This is the perfect freedom of the soul, the 'genuine liberty' in which Wordsworth has learned to see the highest blessing of life; and, while disclaiming for himself the perfect attainment of such a standpoint, he goes on to shew what he owes to his pursuit of a consistent ideal. As he has learned to recognise love as the pervading force of the universe, his early fear of Nature has disappeared, and his imagination, 'Reason in her most exalted mood,' which is inseparable from love and is its active part, has been brought into play; and from the progress of his imaginative faculty he has drawn

> Faith in life endless, the sustaining thought
> Of human Being, Eternity, and God.

47. **the shore**] I.e. of the ocean of mist.

49. **the roar of waters**] See note on *Prelude*, selection v, 20, 21 (p. 173 above).

VIII. DOROTHY WORDSWORTH AND COLERIDGE

From book XIV, 232–301. This apostrophe to Dorothy Wordsworth and to Coleridge follows the passage upon the power of love and imagination, the line of thought of which has been indicated in the introd. note to selection VII, p. 175 above. The progress of Wordsworth's mind towards the attainment of genuine liberty would be incomplete without the recognition of the influence of human love and friendship.

2. **Thanks in sincerest verse**] See especially the tribute to Dorothy's early influence in *The Sparrow's Nest*, written in 1801 (Poems referring to the period of Childhood, No. III), and to its maturity in *Tintern Abbey*, 112–59, pp. 9, 10 above.

8. **genial thought**] Thought in harmony with the special genius or cast of mind which Wordsworth was to develop.

14. **as Milton sings**] See Milton, *P. L.* IX, 490, 491:

> Not terrible, though terror be in love
> And beauty.

See note on *Tintern Abbey*, 71, p. 7 above, for Wordsworth's early association of fear with natural beauty. Milton, *P. L.* I, 781-8, pictures the mingled emotion of a peasant watching the revels of fairies ' by a forest side or fountain ':

> At once with joy and fear his heart rebounds.

17. **too reckless of mild grace**] Too careless of the milder and more graceful aspects of beauty.

22. The image of the bare rock adorned with flowers and shrubs recalls the scene described in *Who fancied what a pretty sight*, p. 33 above.

25–35. Wordsworth refers to the period of his awakening to the true beauty of Nature, described in *Tintern Abbey*, when the love for external beauty had become subordinate to the sense of the spiritual presence which gave it shape and lent the transforming power of imagination to the commonest things.

36. **One whom with thee**] Mary Hutchinson, his wife, the cousin and earliest playmate of the Wordsworths.

36–40. Cf. *She was a phantom of delight*, p. 37 above.

42, 43. See note on *Walton's Book of Lives*, l. 10, p. 162 above. The contrast between the star and the worm, symbolising the heavenly and the earthly, or the ideal and the actual, is found in many poets. See, e.g., the *De contemptu mundi* of Bernard of Cluny:

> Quid datur et quibus? aether egentibus et cruce dignis,
> *Sidera vermibus*, optima sontibus, astra malignis.

Cf. Shelley, *One word is too often profaned*, 13: 'The desire of the moth for the star.'

46. **O capacious Soul**] In *Prelude*, VI, 304, 305, Wordsworth, alluding to Coleridge's learning and eloquence and the philosophical speculations which were to him what the early promptings of 'Nature's living images' were to Wordsworth, characterises his mind as

> unrelentingly possessed by thirst
> Of greatness, love, and beauty.

Here Wordsworth pays his tribute to Coleridge's active exercise of love and sympathy. As a matter of fact, Coleridge's temperament, on his own confession, demanded love and sympathy for itself as a primary requisite. See, e.g., *The Pains of Sleep*, 51, 52:

> To be beloved is all I need,
> And whom I love, I love indeed;

and cf. note on these lines in *Selections from Coleridge* in this series, p. 150. In *Excursion*, II, 46, Wordsworth refers to the 'capacious mind ' of the Wanderer, with its power of universal love for created things.

50. **Thy kindred influence**] Wordsworth refers to his fruitful period of intercourse with Coleridge, described later as

> That summer, under whose indulgent skies,
> Upon smooth Quantock's airy ridge we roved
> Unchecked, or loitered 'mid her sylvan combs.

(*Prelude*, XIV, 396–8.)

55. **The incumbent mystery**] The mystery which always presses on the mind.

57, 58. **a mild Interposition**] The weight of the inexplicable contrast between the actual facts of earthly life and the ideals of the life of the soul became more habitually relieved by a growing content with the common cares and duties of every day, which thus interposed to save the spirit from preoccupation with itself.

63. **The rapture of the hallelujah**] Cf. *Prelude*, II, 409–18:

> Wonder not
> If high the transport, great the joy I felt
> Communing in this sort through earth and heaven
> With every form of creature, as it looked
> Towards the Uncreated with a countenance
> Of adoration, with an eye of love.
> One song they sang, and it was audible,
> Most audible, then, when the fleshly ear,
> O'ercome by humblest prelude of that strain,
> Forgot her functions, and slept undisturbed.

65. **pathetic truth**] The sense of the pathos of daily life, which gives man active sympathy for his fellow-men and prevents absorption in self.

66. **hopeful reason**] Cf. *Ode to Duty*, 55, p. 41 above: ' The confidence of reason give '; and cf. the whole of ll. 51-70 of the present passage with the invocation in ll. 49–56 of the same ode. Man, however lofty his speculations and aims, finds his true content, ' made lowly wise ' in the humble pursuit of the duties which lie about his path.

SELECTIONS FROM THE EXCURSION

The Excursion, begun in 1802, interrupted by the completion of *The Prelude*, and completed 1809–14, was published in 1814, with a dedicatory sonnet to Wordsworth's patron, William, earl of Lonsdale. It was intended to be the second part of 'a philosophical poem, containing views of Man, Nature, and Society; and to be entitled "The Recluse," as having for its principal subject the sensations and opinions of a poet living in retirement.' See introd. note to selections from *The Prelude*, which was to form an introduction to the main poem. A fragment of the first part was written; but the second part proved more congenial to Wordsworth, and, as it formed an independent poem whose interest was not materially affected by the scheme of the first part, it was finished and published separately. The introd. notes to the various selections indicate its general contents, the story of a summer day spent among the hills and valleys of Westmorland. Wordsworth embodied in it his mature reflections upon the relations between man and Nature, with thoughts upon the social conditions of his day and visions of an ampler future. The beauty of style is hardly so well sustained as that of *The Prelude:* its tone is more subdued, and the moral disquisitions of the Wanderer, who plays a large part in it, are apt to become lengthy and didactic; but the careful study of the poem, as is the case with almost all that Wordsworth wrote, reveals its consistent purity and elevation of thought. *The Excursion* is the focus of all his work, in which the unity of aim which controls his miscellaneous poems becomes clearly apparent.

I. THE WANDERER'S BOYHOOD

From *The Excursion*, I (*The Wanderer*), 118–96. Part of the description of the intellectual growth of the Wanderer, whom the author represents himself as meeting at the beginning of the poem. The experiences related are those of Wordsworth himself and form an epitome of those described and analysed in *The*

Prelude. See especially selection I, pp. 77–82 above. The Wanderer is depicted as a Scot, the son of a poor farmer 'upon the hills of Athol,' a district which Wordsworth visited in 1803.

8. **minster clock**] Cf. Tennyson, *The Gardener's Daughter*, 38: 'The windy clanging of the minster clock.'

16. **terror**] The emotion constantly referred to by Wordsworth as predominating in his early communion with Nature. See, e.g., selection IX from *The Prelude*, 14, 15, p. 89 above, and his account of his wanderings by night in the hills, *Prelude*, I, 312–25.

19. **greatness**] The cardinal example of the impression left by 'great objects' upon Wordsworth's mind is the

huge peak, black and huge,
As if with voluntary power instinct

of *Prelude*, I, 378, 379 (selection I, 39, 40, p. 78 above).

22. **Perplexed the bodily sense**] Such impressions of hidden power stamped themselves on the mind with the clearness of images derived from concrete shapes, and raised doubts of the line of division which separates concrete objects, apprehended by the senses, from abstract objects, perceived only by the mind. These are the 'obstinate questionings' referred to in *Intimations of Immortality*, 141–7, p. 49 above: see note on l. 141, p. 143 above.

27. **character**] The shape, like handwriting, which impressions leave upon the mind.

40–5. Either because he possessed a special and individual power of intellectual vision, by which he directly recognised the unseen; or because his active power of creating images for himself exercised an undivided sway over his mind, and affected his fancy; or because thought had so gained the mastery over him that his own ebbing and flowing thoughts reflected themselves in all the objects round him.

54. For the influence of books upon Wordsworth see *Prelude*, V, especially his account, ll. 460 sqq., of the abstract of *The Arabian Nights* which he possessed at Hawkshead. The actual volumes mentioned here cannot be identified with cer-

tainty; but the minister's library would probably have contained a copy of Foxe's *Acts and Monuments*, popularly known as the *Book of Martyrs*, the first English version of which was published in 1563, and some of the miscellaneous literature relating to the Covenanters.

58. **the Covenant**] The Solemn League and Covenant, sworn to by the Scots on 1 March, 1637–8, pledged the nation to extirpate prelacy and establish the simplest form of presbyterian church government. After the accession of Charles II, the Covenanters were harassed and persecuted. Their sufferings became the subject of many biographies and pamphlets, on which Sir Walter Scott drew freely in *Old Mortality*. Wordsworth may have been thinking of such books as Patrick Walker's lives of Cameron and other Covenanters, which Scott read in his boyhood.

62. **left half-told**] Cf. Milton, *Il Penseroso*, 109:

> Or call up him that left half told
> The story of Cambuscan bold.

65. **dire faces, figures dire**] Cf. Milton, *P. L.* II, 628: 'Gorgons and Hydras, and Chimeras dire.'

69. See notes on *Tintern Abbey*, 71, pp. 110, 111 above, and on l. 16 above.

76. **his intense conceptions**] I.e. the conceptions derived from 'the active power of fastening images' upon the brain: see ll. 26–31 above.

II. THE VALLEY OF BLEA TARN

From book II (*The Solitary*), 319–48. This part of the poem describes a walk taken by the author and the Wanderer. Their course leads them up a wide valley, which can be readily identified with Great Langdale, to the S.W. of Grasmere. On the way, the Wanderer tells the main outlines of the story of the Solitary, whom he proposes to visit, and, with this purpose, turns aside to cross the fells into the remote valley where the Solitary has taken up his abode. The route described is that between

Great Langdale and Little Langdale, which lies to the south. The 'steep ascent' (l. 6) climbs the fell-side opposite the Langdale Pikes and the fall of Dungeon Ghyll. The 'dreary plain' at the top opens suddenly into the valley in which lies Blea Tarn, the 'liquid pool' of l. 20. The stream from Blea Tarn falls into Little Langdale, where it meets the Brathay.

7. **huge hill tops**] The Langdale Pikes are immediately across the valley to the north: westward are the lofty summits which culminate in Scafell; while to the south, Wetherlam, the 'black and huge' peak which, as seen from Esthwaite, had terrified Wordsworth in his boyhood, stands out conspicuously among the mountains of Coniston and Tilberthwaite.

11. **A lowly vale**] An instance of the poetical figure known as Anadiplosis, by which the word or phrase which concludes one line is repeated with emphatic effect at the beginning of the next, usually with slight variation. Cf. Milton, *P. L.* VII, 25, 26:

Though fall'n on evil days,
On evil days though fall'n, and evil tongues.

uplifted high] The valley of Blea Tarn is one of those higher valleys, set directly among the hills, the streams from which feed the main valleys at the foot of the hills.

13. **from eldest time**] Cf. *Excursion*, III, 301: 'Of what from eldest time we have been told.'

by wish of theirs] Note Wordsworth's characteristic attribution of human will to the mountains.

19. **treeless nook**] Since Wordsworth wrote, trees have been planted beside the lake, sheltering the 'moorland house' from the west wind.

24. **many thrifty years**] Cf. the description of the thrifty husbandry of the Lake country peasants in *Michael*, pp. 13–16 above.

26. **single in his domain**] I.e. the only bird there.

29, 30. For this beautiful description of the cuckoo's song, cf. *To the Cuckoo*, 5–8, and *The Solitary Reaper*, 13–16, pp. 22, 34 above. The quiet and faithful picture of the scene is heightened by this final touch of imagination.

III. THE LANGDALE PIKES

From book II, 688–725. The two peaks which give occasion to 'this high-wrought strain of rapture' are the Langdale Pikes, the rocky tops of which overlook the fells among which Blea Tarn lies. There are few mountains in the Lake country which have so striking a shape: there is a magnificent view of them, across the intervening valley of Great Langdale, from the brow of the hill which the author and the Wanderer had climbed on their way to the Solitary's cottage.

11. **dashing shores**] Shores against which water dashes.

18. **stream and headlong flood**] Cf. note on *Prelude*, selection v, 20, 21 (p. 173 above). The Great Langdale beck flows down the valley of Mickleden at the foot of the pikes, and two of its tributaries, on one of which is the waterfall of Dungeon Ghyll, take their source in these mountains.

23. **a harmony**] The perpetual change of light and shade and colour upon the mountains gives them a continually varying expression which seems to be the visible sign of a hidden intelligence and activity, responsive to every call of the atmosphere. Their silence is that of a mind always at work which communicates its harmonious influence to the watcher.

IV. THE FRENCH REVOLUTION

From book III, 706-58. Part of the narrative told by the Solitary. The death of his children, followed by that of his wife, led him into the 'abstraction' referred to in l. 1, in which he sought to unravel the mysteries of time and eternity. The fall of the Bastille and the dreams of liberty to which it gave rise awakened him from these speculations to take part in the revolutionary movement. Wordsworth describes his enthusiasm from the personal experiences detailed in *The Prelude*. In the sequel, the

Solitary, like Wordsworth, was disenchanted of his hopes. Consoling himself for a time with a wayward course of living, in which license of conduct took the place of disinterested zeal for liberty, he determined to leave Europe and seek the home of freedom in America. Here again, even in the remote west, he found the contradiction between ideals and facts too much for him, and at last settled down to the solitary life in which the author and the Wanderer find him. The present passage sums up the attraction which the French revolution in its earlier stages offered to ardent minds, such as those of Wordsworth and Coleridge, and illustrates the important influence which it exercised upon the Romatic movement in literature.

4. **the dread Bastille**] The Bastille, the royal stronghold on the east side of Paris, long used as a state prison, was destroyed by the mob on 14 July, 1789.

9. **a golden palace**] Figurative. The fall of the Bastille was the symbol of the end of tyranny, and a promise of hope to the framers of the new Constitution, which had already been taken in hand by the Constituent assembly. The Declaration of the Rights of Man, which was intended to be a preface to the Constitution, was agreed upon on 27 Aug. The Solitary's conviction that a new golden age was beginning is typical of the child-like confidence which possessed men's minds after the sudden victory over despotism. See *Prelude*, VI, 339–41:

> But Europe at that time was thrilled with joy,
> France standing on the top of golden hours,
> And human nature seeming born again.

11. **mild paternal sway**] The monarchy of France, under the new order of things, became constitutional. On 4 August, 1789, the Constituent assembly passed a number of decrees which abolished the feudal system in France, and Louis XVI was proclaimed the Restorer of French liberty. The headlong haste with which the whole of the ancient order of things was destroyed in a night was naturally responsible for the anarchy which followed.

14. **the blind mist**] The fruitless speculations in which the Solitary had lost himself before this sudden awakening.

18, 19. The prospect of a reign of universal peace embodied in this prophecy was soon disappointed. France found herself at war with Europe, and her successful efforts to repel her enemies led her into a long war of conquest.

21. **The tree of Liberty**] The anniversary of the fall of the Bastille was kept in Paris by a national feast of federation, at which a general oath was taken in approval of the decrees of the Assembly. Such federal feasts were kept throughout France, and trees emblematic of liberty were planted in each town and commune.

27. **mutual and reflected wealth**] Well-being, moral and material, shared by every member of the community, all goods being held in common, and every man communicating his store of wealth and happiness to his less fortunate neighbours.

30, 31. He was consoled for the loss of his wife by his joy in a regenerated society, and for that of his children by the unsubstantial hopes which seemed to him realities.

41. **sober conclave**] Numerous political associations were founded in England during the epoch of the French revolution, to further the principles of social reform which had worked the great change in France. The most important of these were the Constitutional and Corresponding societies, the second of which, organised on a democratic basis, held mass meetings such as those mentioned in ll. 44-7. The Constitutional society came to an end in 1794; but the Corresponding society, which gathered strength after the failure of the government to sustain the prosecution of the English revolutionary leaders, did not come to an end until the aggressive policy of the Directory had turned English sympathy against France.

51. **Saturnian rule**] The reign of Saturn, before Jupiter overthrew the old order of Olympus, was the traditional golden age of peace and prosperity. Cf. Vergil, *Ecl.* IV, 6: 'Iam redit et virgo, redeunt Saturnia regna.'

V. NATURAL RELIGION IN GREECE

From book IV (*Despondency Corrected*), 851–87. In this book the Wanderer endeavours to impress upon the Solitary the dangers of the morbid avoidance of his fellow-creatures and indifference to human feeling which he cultivates. In pointing out the influences which bring peace of mind to man, he lays stress upon religious feeling, which, in all ages of the world and under a variety of forms, has called man to a higher perception of life. In these lines he shews

The face which rural solitude might wear
To the unenlightened swains of pagan Greece,

who invested the powers of Nature presiding over their own occupations with kindred interests, and gave to each visible object a divine personality. Previously, in ll. 718 sqq., he has touched upon the same subject: the gods of Greece were imaged in metal and stone and surrounded with superstitious legends, but, in spite of the influence of the senses upon worship, the presence of one divine spirit was felt to animate the face of Nature, and each natural object became a manifestation of its power.

1. **that fair clime**] Greece.

9. **a beardless Youth**] Apollo or Phoebus, the personification of the sun and the god of music.

11. **nightly**] By night. Cf. Milton, *P. L.* II, 642: 'Ply stemming nightly toward the pole.'

15. **a beaming Goddess**] Artemis or Cynthia, sister of Apollo, and goddess of the moon, represented as a huntress with an attendant train of nymphs.

16. **lawn**] A clearing in a forest.

20. **Glance rapidly**] The moon and stars seem to move through the sky, as they are hidden by and emerge from the flying clouds drifting beneath them. For 'glance' cf. the quotation in note on l. 26 below.

23. **The Naiad**] The nymph supposed to have her local habitation in each stream or fountain.

26. **Oreads**] Mountain nymphs. Cf. *Excursion*, vi, 829:

Oread or Dryad glancing through the shade
What time the hunter's earliest horn is heard
Startling the golden hills.

27. **Zephyrs**] The westerly breezes personified.

36. **Pan**] See note on the sonnet *Composed by the side of Grasmere Lake*, 12, p. 137 above. Pan and his attendant Satyrs were represented with the horns, hoofs and beards of goats.

VI. THE INWARD POWER OF THE SOUL

From book iv, 1058–77. The Wanderer has just contrasted wilful and self-centred solitude with the seclusion of the soul in which the call of duty is obeyed and humility takes the place of pride, producing true content and enjoyment with freedom from apprehension of the future.

1–5. The soul, man's immortal part, possesses an inherent virtue or power, the capacity of triumphing over the material circumstances which seem to hinder it. Such impediments, which threaten to hide and darken the soul's natural brightness, thus appear in their true form as foils which set off and enhance the splendour of the soul superior to their influence. Cf. Milton, *Comus*, 373–5:

Virtue could see to do what virtue would
By her own radiant light, though sun and moon
Were in the flat sea sunk.

2. **interpositions**] Cf. *Prelude*, selection ix, 57, 58 (p. 91 above): 'a mild Interposition.' These interpositions are the doubts and anxieties which interpose themselves between the soul and the proper objects of its contemplation.

4. **Contingencies of pomp**] Mere accidents which attend the soul's unclouded progress. 'Pomp' literally means 'procession,' as in Milton, *P. L.* vii, 564: 'While the bright pomp

ascended jubilant.' In the present case the word refers at once to the triumphant progress of the soul whose inner virtue is superior to obstacles, and to the splendour associated with such progress.

10. **umbrage**] See note on *Yew-Trees*, 22, p. 128 above. For this passage, cf. *Excursion*, VII, 598, 599:

> Light birch, aloft upon the horizon's edge,
> A veil of glory for the ascending moon.

14. **virtue**] *Virtus* is literally the quality which is proper to a man (*vir*), manliness, courage. It is the specific name for that inner power of the soul which Wordsworth describes, the power which finds an incentive to its exercise in 'the encumbrances of mortal life.' For 'virtue' in the sense of 'active power,' cf. St Luke vi, 19: 'there went virtue out of him, and healed them all.' In the ancient division of the angels into three hierarchies, the second order of the middle hierarchy was that of the Virtues, to whom was appropriated the active ministry of working: nothing, it is said in *The Golden Legend*, was impossible for them 'to execute which that is commanded to them, for to them is given power to do all things difficult which be pertaining to divine mystery, and therefore it is attributed to them to do miracles.' The ordinary sense of 'virtue' is applied to the moral qualities which are the manifestations of this secret faculty of the soul in its active employment.

18. **nay, from guilt**] The soul finds material for the use of its power even in contemplating and experiencing the worst evils of daily life. Similarly, one of the cardinal doctrines of Browning's poetry is that the existence of evil in the world is as a mere foil to the splendour of goodness; but he goes further to the conclusion that, without the contrast of evil, goodness would be too dazzling for mortal eyes.

20. **palpable oppressions**] Oppressions which affect the senses. The justice of Heaven, while allowing the soul to be attacked by despair, provides even in this extremity an opportunity for the triumph of its inner strength.

VII. THE VOICES OF NATURE

From book IV, 1156–87. The Wanderer is expatiating upon the power of the universe to act as a medium between man and the invisible, just as in a shell, when its opening is placed to the ear, are heard

> Murmurings, whereby the monitor expressed
> Mysterious union with its native sea.

In like manner, the soul finds in the sights and sounds of Nature, received by the senses, echoes of ' the immortal sea ' of eternity, from which, as set forth in *Intimations of Immortality*, its being has proceeded.

2. **a shock of awful consciousness**] Cf. the ' gentle shock of mild surprise ' in *Prelude*, selection v, 19, p. 85 above.

5. **circumambient**] Surrounding. The evening mists, descending upon the crags, from the roof of a temple of which the crags are the walls.

10. **What if these**] See selection II, 26–30, for the absence or rarity of birds in the bleak mountain-valley of Blea Tarn.

23. **the solitary raven**] See introd. note on *To Joanna*, and note on ll. 56–66, pp. 118, 119, 120, 121 above.

VIII. THE DEAF DALESMAN

From book VII, 395–481. Books V–IX of *The Excursion* are the account of a visit paid by the author, with the Wanderer and Solitary, to a more populous valley, where they are welcomed by the vicar of the parish, an old friend of the Wanderer. In books VI and VII the Pastor holds a dialogue in the churchyard with his visitors and tells them the stories of some of those who lie buried there. These character sketches have a pathos and a sympathy with rustic life which are Wordsworth's own peculiar property, and the instance given here is perhaps the most striking of such ' clear images '

> Of nature's unambitious underwood,
> And flowers that prosper in the shade.

Its style should be compared with that of the picture given in

Michael, selection I, pp. 13–16 above: it has a similar quietude and similar fitness of language to a homely subject, blended with an exalted sense of the stern grandeur of the natural setting of the tale. The narratives in this part of *The Excursion* naturally provoke a comparison with those told by Crabbe in *The Parish Register* and other poems; but Crabbe, while possessing gifts of humour and epigrammatic brevity which form a remarkable contrast to Wordsworth's unrelieved seriousness and occasional prolixity, took a less optimistic view of human nature and lacked Wordsworth's sense of the sublime encouragement afforded to man by his natural environment. The churchyard is that of Grasmere, and the narratives are drawn from personal reminiscences of the neighbourhood.

6. **a plain blue stone**] Of the local slate.

11. **The bird of dawn**] Cf. Gray, *Elegy*, 19, 20, 'The cock's shrill clarion,' etc. The cock and the cuckoo (l. 14) were the only birds whose voices were heard in the Solitary's valley: see selection II, 26–30, p. 95 above. As the dialogue of the Pastor and the Wanderer was intended to rouse the Solitary from his self-concentrated retirement, an intentional contrast is probably implied between the privileges allowed to him and denied to the dalesman, who, in spite of his isolation from the sounds of earth, retained content and fortitude.

14. **vernal**] Cf. *The Tables turned*, 21, p. 4 above.

23. **the solace of his own pure thoughts**] Cf. Milton, *Comus*, 381, 382:

> He that has light within his own clear breast
> May sit i' the centre, and enjoy bright day.

40. **independent love**] Voluntary love, alloyed by no sense of dependence upon another person.

52. **His introverted spirit**] His spirit, forced, through his deafness, to inward communion with itself.

59, 60. See Hebrews xii, 23: 'the spirits of just men made perfect'; and Wisdom iii, 1: 'the souls of the righteous are in the hand of God, and there shall no torment touch them.'

67. **slow-varying**] Slow to alter, alluding to the patient fixity of expression habitual to the faces of the deaf, which relaxes slowly in proportion to their gradual comprehension of events round them.

IX. SUNSET AND SUMMER HAZE

From book IX, 590–608. The concluding scene of the poem, from a hill-slope on the shore of the lake opposite the village. All its personages are assembled here, and the sunset gives occasion to the Pastor's hymn of ' holy transport ' to the ' Eternal Spirit! universal God!' with which the day closes. After this ' vesper-service ' the party cross the lake silently ' under a faded sky,' as the stars come out, and separate, the Solitary returning to his valley with new hope derived from communion with his fellows and their lessons of sympathy. This beautiful picture of a quiet and hazy evening sky transfigured by the power of sunset should be compared with the magnificent vision of full sunlight breaking through cloud and mist after a storm on the mountains, in *Excursion*, II, 829–69, and with the stanzas *Composed upom an evening of extraordinary splendour and beauty.*

6. **the dense air**] The thick haze at the end of a hot summer day, hiding the sun. Cf. the Latin *spissus aër*, the dense atmosphere, contrasted in Ovid, *Mett.* I, 23, with the *liquidum caelum*, the clear firmament.

9. **pierced**] I.e. the little clouds were pierced by the rays of the setting sun.

16. **the unapparent fount of glory**] The sun itself, still unseen, but communicating its brightness to the whole sky.

18. **the liquid deep**] The lake below, reflecting the glory of the sky.

INDEX TO NOTES

Lightning Source UK Ltd.
Milton Keynes UK
UKOW02f1101280916

283999UK00001B/2/P